DIGITAL ARCHITECTURE
NEW APPROACHES

LINKS

DIGITAL ARCHITECTURE: NEW APPROACHES
Edition 2013

Author: Dimitris Kottas
Graphic design and production: Cuboctaedro & Oriol Vallès
Cover design: Oriol Vallès, graphic designer
Cover image: contributed by upgrade.studio
Text: contributed by the architects, edited by Emily McBride and Naomi Ferguson

© LinksBooks
Jonqueres, 10, 1-5
08003 Barcelona, España
Tel.: +34-93-301-21-99
info@linksbooks.net
www.linksbooks.net

DIGITAL ARCHITECTURE
NEW APPROACHES

LINKS

Index

Introduction

This book presents the latest developments in the field of architecture as it has been reshaped by the use of digital technologies. Digital architecture has been defined by a broad range of events and technologies that go beyond the use of architectural software. These include the proliferation and great availability of CNC technologies, the possibility of designing parametrically with the use of many different programs, the use of algorithms and simulations of natural and biological processes as morphogenetic strategies, the development of hardware and software for interactive applications as well as the exploration of digital imagine and other techniques developed in fields remote from architecture.

The works selected for the book come from young architects who have found digital media to be their natural environment. These are experimental and daring projects that include urban areas and express the creative and imaginative potential of a new generation of architects.

The book includes small-scale projects that demonstrate the use of digital technologies in the construction process, technologies that are available to any designer (and also to students) and are not limited to the higher budgets of large engineering firms. Other projects make use of computer programing in architectural design. The architects presented here do not limit themselves in the use of the ready-made forms of commercial software but explore the possibilities of creating forms through algorithmic processes.

Finally, there are projects which go beyond, seeking to bind sustainability to technology, though these are two terms which often are not used together. The proposals contained here have found solutions in the intelligent application of technology.

Given that digital technologies evolve and overlap, it is clear that we cannot wait for digital architecture to become a stable discipline with formal rules and techniques. It is, and likely will continue to be, a field of experimentation and exploration.

Digital Form-Finding

We have seen how parametric processes create an open-ended design methodology where many outcomes are possible. However in many cases the goal can be the design of a single project that needs to be constructed and stabilized at some point. Especially in the earlier days of digital design the parametric process was presented as an objective method for reaching an optimum final outcome based on the given conditions. This attempt to remove the subjective factor from the design process and present issues of social space construction as objective mechanistic processes has been criticized by many. Today it is understood that although very powerful, parametric design remains a procedure where subjectivity is inserted in many stages. Younger designers have found this to be a merit of parametric design that provides room for inspiration, expression and personalization.

From the setting of the problem to the selection of the parameters, the orchestrating of their algorithmic interaction and the selection of one among the many possible outcomes, parametric design is filled with moments where subjectivity, knowledge and inspiration are called to guide the process. Form-finding strategies have become therefore an important aspect of digital architecture, one that younger designers are eager to explore, not to reach an absolute objectivity, but to find a personal voice and embrace difference and unpredictability.

OTA+, the designers of the **Off/Grid House,** had little interest in repeating the design aesthetic of typical off-grid and sustainable houses. Rather, they decided to invent an entirely new formal language using an evolutionary process of formal development, testing and selection. They began by producing an extensive catalog of digital models, each offering unique formal and spatial opportunities. Each step in the process and its formal consequence was documented and represented in its totality, which allowed them to evaluate and compare the differences between each form at any stage of development. The process continued until a critical threshold was reached, past which the form lost all spatial potential.

By extracting the sequence of parameters that produced a form, or even a specific part of a form, the designers could recreate particular moments that were selected for the house. Variation of the parameters within the limits defined by the selected digital model allowed them to fine-tune the form, accommodate the functional requirements of the house, and meet specific requirements necessary for an off-grid house to work. In the event that a part was formally incompatible with its neighbor, they varied the appropriate parameters to alleviate geometric conflicts.

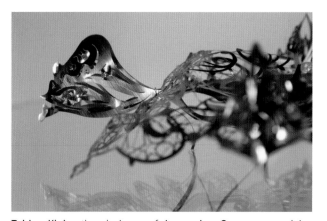

The Inverted Monument is part of **Kokkugia's** ongoing research into Behavioral Design Methodologies. These methodologies operate through Multi-Agent algorithms to generate a landscape with a differentiated field of intensities, which culminates in an intense aggregation - the inverted monument. The non-linear interaction of the agents is used to navigate a field of varying charge, negotiating between their own swarm logic and a field of external influences.

Tobias Klein, the designer of **Immersive Ornament** explains his understanding of the role of the architect in the digital age: *"The emergence of computer-aided design is a key player in stretching artifice to its extremes, leading on the one hand to a parametric process-driven generative architecture and on the other to a new role of architects as the creator-craftsman able to reunite architecture as an interplay between techne (art) and poiesis (craftsmanship) - counterarguing a modernism of functionality. I work and operate within a CAD/CAM liberated environment but do not consider myself solely and epistemologically interested in a parametric accountancy of the computational potential and manufactured customization and efficiency driven optimization, but in a cultural amalgamation between tool and idea embedded in specifics of site and narration."*

OTA+

Off/Grid House

The Off/Grid House project is located just outside of Albuquerque, New Mexico in a private community surrounded by the Cibola National Forest. Despite being only a few hundred yards from Albuquerque, no utilities are allowed to pass through the Forest to connect the site to the city grid. Consequently, the house was designed to be entirely self-sustaining and off-grid.

The designers had little interest in repeating the design aesthetic of typical off-grid and sustainable houses. Rather, they decided to invent an entirely new formal language using an evolutionary process of formal development, testing and selection. They began by producing an extensive catalog of digital models, each offering unique formal and spatial opportunities. Each step in the process and its formal consequence was documented and represented in its totality, which allowed them to evaluate and compare the differences between each form at any stage of development. The process continued until a critical threshold was reached, past which the form lost all spatial potential.

By extracting the sequence of parameters that produced a form, or even a specific part of a form, the designers could recreate particular moments that were selected for the house. Variation of the parameters within the limits defined by the selected digital model allowed them to fine-tune the form, accommodate the functional requirements of the house, and meet specific requirements necessary for an off-grid house to work. In the event that a part was formally incompatible with its neighbor, they varied the appropriate parameters to alleviate geometric conflicts.

The seams between neighboring parts not only provided dimensional tolerance between incompatible geometries, they also became opportunities in and of themselves. Seams were activated as either enclosed space to be shared by adjacent programs and foster new associations of use, or left as branching voids to help circulate light and air. Though unexpected, the result was one of greater programmatic coordination and connection to the site and natural resources, a necessity when building an off-grid house.

Though the process was non-linear and the cataloguing of form was restarted when necessary, the designers reached a point, a function of time and project scale, at which they began to evaluate the digital models according to their potential for architecture. Of course, the basis for evaluation and selection of form requires considerable attention. When designing an off-grid house, as this project required, the programmatic and spatial requirements have an additional layer of complexity. To graphically represent these requirements, they developed a program narrative: a diagrammatic description of information that predicates the organization of the program and its relationship to the context, including views, circulation, use, adjacency and the application of environmental control systems. This information was embedded through a set of illustrated codes. By changing the shape, scale, color, line type and line weight of each code, they could identify the type and amount of impact it had on a particular space. Ultimately, the program index became a map for how they began to evaluate and test the extensive catalog of forms that they produced at the start of the process. The forms that were both spatially provocative and best matched the needs identified in the codified index were actuated in the final house design. Requirements that were seemingly incompatible were matched with equally complex models, capable of handling multiple needs simultaneously. What started as a willful exploration of formal and spatial models subsisting in a state of limbo, became a realized set of integrated units indispensible to the project.

Design: Kory Bieg and Alexa Getting
Location: Albuquerque, New Mexico, USA

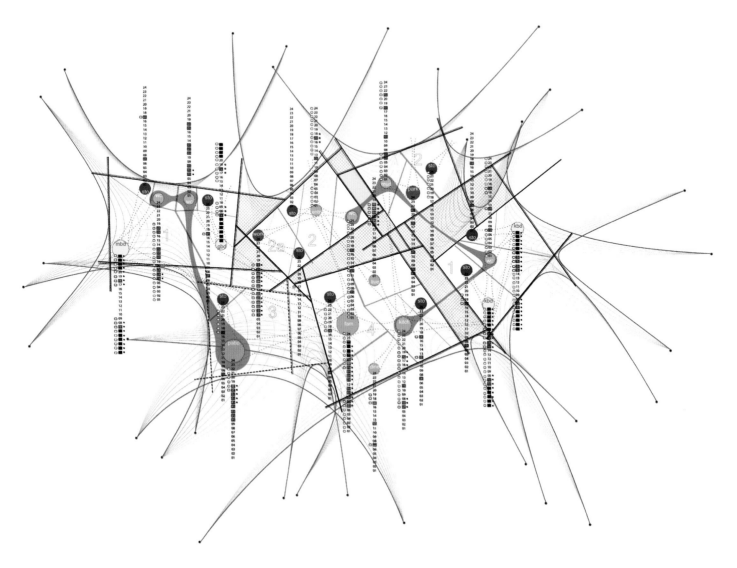

1	Sleep / dress	::::	Circulation
2	Receive	●	Comfort zone required
2a	Work	○	Comfort zone occasional
3	Exterior entertain	▥	Upright movement
4	Entertain / dine	▤	Lounge / lay
	Views	▦	Combination
	Sun penetration	■	Sleeping / static
	Utility sharing	▫	Electrical light needed
	Light wells	▫	Electrical light occasional

Operation	Variable	Value
Create plane	Length	10' 10''
	Width	10' 10'
	Segments	1
Create Spline		
Add Edit Poly		
Select Polygons		
Extrude Along Spl	Segments	20
	Tapper Amount	-1.0
	Taper Curve	2.0
Symmetry	Axis	X
Add Edit Poly		
Select Polygons		
Bridge	Segments	10
	Taper	1.0
	Twist 1	1.0
Bend	Angle	140.0
	Axis	Y
Twist	Angle	227.0
	Axis	X
Mesh Smooth	Itterations	3

Operation	Variable	Value
Create plane	Length	10' 10''
	Width	10' 10'
	Segments	3
Create Spline		
Add Edit Poly		
Select Polygons		
Extrude Along Spl	Segments	16
	Tapper Amount	0.85
	Taper Curve	4.0
Bend	Angle	141
	Axis	Z
Twist	Angle	109.5
	Axis	Z
Stretch	Stretch	1.0
	Amplify	-1.8
	Axis	Z
Symmetry	Axis	X
Symmetry	Axis	Z
Stretch	Stretch	-0.4
	Axis	Z
Mesh Smooth	Itterations	3

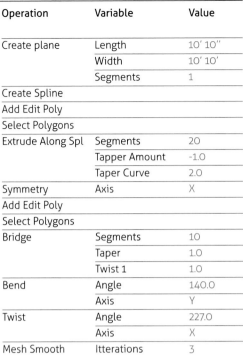

Operation	Variable	Value
Create plane	Length	12' 10''
	Width	12' 10'
	Segments	4
Relax	Value	1.0
	Itterations	3
Add Edit Poly		
Select Vertices		
Chamfer	Amount	6''
Select Polygons		
Bridge	Segments	5
	Taper	-3.0
	Bias	-6.0
Symmetry	Axis	X
Spherify	Percent	28.0
Twist	Angle	77.0
	Axis	X
Mesh Smooth	Itterations	3
Symmetry	Axis	Y
Noise	Strength X	-14' 0''
	Strength Y	33' 2''
	Strength Z	34' 6''

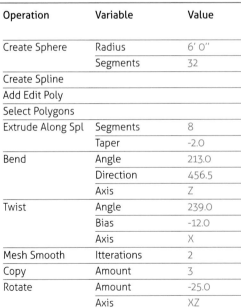
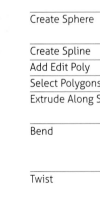

Operation	Variable	Value
Create Sphere	Radius	6' 0''
	Segments	32
Create Spline		
Add Edit Poly		
Select Polygons		
Extrude Along Spl	Segments	8
	Taper	-2.0
Bend	Angle	213.0
	Direction	456.5
	Axis	Z
Twist	Angle	239.0
	Bias	-12.0
	Axis	X
Mesh Smooth	Itterations	2
Copy	Amount	3
Rotate	Amount	-25.0
	Axis	XZ

Operation	Variable	Value
Create Torus Knot	Radius	3' 11"
	Segments	120
	Cross-section	2"
	Sides	12
Relax	Value	0.5
	Iterations	1
Push	Value	6"
Twist	Angle	-183.5
	Axis	Z
Mesh Smooth	Iterations	2
FFD	3×3×3	
Copy	Amount	3
Rotate	Amount	3
	Axis	XY

Operation	Variable	Value
Create Plane	Length	40' 0'
	Width	42' 5"
	Segments	4
Bend	Angle	-21.0
	Axis	Y
Twist	Angle	140.0
	Axis	Z
Mirror	Axis	ZX
	Offset	10' 3"
Bend	Angle	145.0
	Axis	Y
Mesh Smooth	Iterations	2
Add Edit Poly		
Select Polygons		
Insert	Amount	5"
Mesh Smooth	Iterations	1

Operation	Variable	Value
Create Plane	Length	53' 3"
	Width	99' 1"
	Segments	4
Add Edit Poly		
Select Polygons		
Bevel	Height	48' 9"
	Outline	-2' 1"
Mesh Smooth	Iterations	3
Bend	Angle	195.5
	Direction	83.5
	Axis	Y
Twist	Angle	97.0
	Bias	-15.0
	Axis	Z
FFD	3×3×3	
Symmetry	Axis	Z
Twist	Angle	232.0
	Axis	Z

Operation	Variable	Value
Create Box	Length	11' 0"
	Width	11' 6"
	Height	9' 6"
	Segments	15
Create Torus Knot	Radius	3' 3"
	Segments	314
	Cross-Sections	2' 2"
	Sides	79
Boolean	Box-Torus Knot	
Twist	Angle	79.5
	Axis	Z
Ripple	Amp 1	1' 10"
	Amp 2	10"
	Wave Length	6' 4"
Stretch	Stretch	-0.7
	Axis	Z
FFD	3×3×3	
Mesh Smooth	Iterations	3

Operation	Variable	Value
Create Gengon	Sides	5
	Radius	5' 6"
	Height	2' 9"
Bend	Angle	23.0
	Direction	2409.0
	Axis	Z
Spherify	Percent	58.0
Bend	Angle	-9.0
	Direction	48.0
	Axis	Z
Push	Value	3' 6"
Stretch	Stretch	1.0
	Axis	Y
Twist	Angle	317.0
	Axis	Y
Turbosmooth	Iterations	3
Shell	Outer Amount	1/2"

Operation	Variable	Value
Create Plane	Length	40' 2"
	Width	77' 0"
	Segments	4
Bend	Angle	196.5
	Direction	47.5
	Axis	X
Twist	Angle	204.0
	Bias	14.0
	Axis	Y
Add Edit Poly		
Select Polygons	Delete	
Mirror	Axis	YZ
	Offset	4' 10"
Bend	Angle	138.0
	Axis	X
Symmetry	Axis	Y
FFD	3×3×3	
Shell	Outer Amount	2"
Turbosmooth	Iterations	3

Operation	Variable	Value
Create Plane	Length	75' 0"
	Width	70' 9"
	Segments	4
Bend	Angle	212.0
	Direction	21.5
	Axis	X
Mirror	Axis	ZX
	Offset	1' 5"
Mirror	Axis	XY
	Offset	-15' 0"
Stretch	Stretch	1.0
	Amplify	-1.3
	Axis	X
Twist	Angle	118.5
	Axis	Z
Add Edit Poly		
Select Polygons		
Scale	Amount	115.0
Lattice	Radius	2"
	Segments	1
	Sides	4

Operation	Variable	Value
Create Box	Length	9' 7"
	Width	9' 2"
	Height	6' 10"
	Segments	3
Add Edit Poly		
Select Edges		
Chamfer	Amount	9"
	Segments	1
Select Polygons		
Bevel	Height	7"
	Outline	3"
Insert	Amount	3"
FFD	3×3×3	
Mesh Smooth	Iterations	2
Twist	Angle	127.5
	Axis	Y
Bend	Angle	-185.0
	Axis	Z
Mesh Smooth	Iterations	2

Kokkugia | Roland Snooks

The Inverted Monument | Kiev

This speculative project reconsiders the monument as object, instead positing the formation of an immersive space of remembrance, a space that emerges from the landscape and is carved from within a somber stone monolith – an inverted monument.

Rather than the reductive, singular, top-down imposition of form, this project explores the emergence of a space, rich with intricate detail, reflecting the culmination of individual differences within a multitude. The memorial is designed through the use of complex non-linear systems in which coherent order and space emerge from interactions at a local scale.

This project is part of Kokkugia's ongoing research into Behavioral Design Methodologies. These methodologies operate through Multi-Agent algorithms to generate a landscape with a differentiated field of intensities, which culminates in an intense aggregation - the inverted monument. The non-linear interaction of the agents is used to navigate a field of varying charge, negotiating between their own swarm logic and a field of external influences. The project is concerned both with the emergence of a figure from a field as well as the dissolution of the figure into abstraction. The space of remembrance within the inverted monument is cast from bronze and generated through the interaction of agent-based components. At a local level the component has no base state, but instead adapts to its conditions. Consequently while local moments of periodicity may occur, its constant shifting of state triggered by local relationships resists a definitive reading of the component.

The component logic of this carved space is polyscalar: self-similar algorithmic agents operate across scales to form a continuous tectonic, where the legibility of discrete tectonic hierarchies dissolve. Through this disintegration of hierarchy a new set of intensive effects emerge.

Design: Kokkugia | Roland Snooks
Design team: Roland Snooks, M. Casey Rehm, Fleet Hower, William Bryant Netter

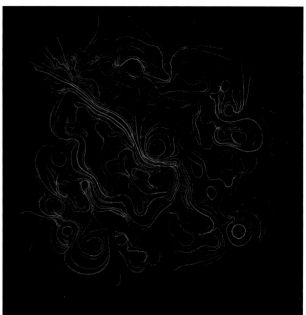

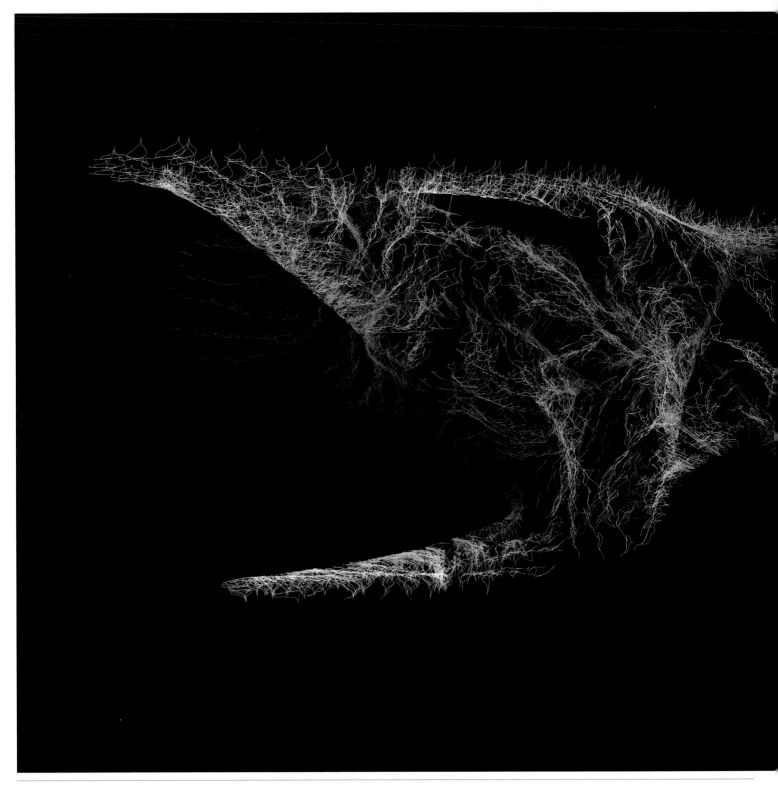

EMERGENT | Tom Wiscombe & KOKKUGIA | Roland Snooks

Yeosu Oceanic Pavilion

This project is the result of collaboration between Wiscombe and Snooks, intended to capitalize on both shared sensibilities and individual expertise. It is an exploration of messy computation in the sense that the project is the result of moving in and out of the realms of designing and scripting. It represents a loose, open-ended way of working that biases effects over self-justifying processes.

The Pavilion is intended to be the centerpiece for the Yeosu 2010 Expo, a space which celebrates the ocean as a living organism and the co-existence of human culture and ocean ecosystems. In our design proposal, the building object and its territory enter into a feedback loop. The role of the architect is expanded to include the active re-organization of matters and energies around and underneath the building, where the species selects its environment as much as the environment selects its species.

The building is based on an aggregation of soft membrane bubbles merged together with a hard monocoque shell. The two systems are characterized by patterns of surface articulation which are specific to their materiality. Nevertheless, features tend to migrate, hybridize and become redundant.

Deep pleats and mega-armatures that create structural stiffness are generally associated with the fiber-composite shell, while fine, double-pleated Air-beams spread over and stabilize the vaulted ETFE membranes. Micro-armatures (a.k.a. 'Mohawks') transgress thresholds between shell and membrane, creating structural and ornamental continuity between systems.

Color is used to visually intensify transformations in structural behavior (for instance mega-armatures tend towards purple/pink while Mohawks tend towards orange/yellow). Nevertheless, color gradients are neither 100% indexical nor are they completely smooth; they are coherent yet glitchy. No longer secondary to form, color becomes critical in an overall ecology of features.

Designers: EMERGENT & KOKKUGIA
Design Team EMERGENT: Tom Wiscombe, David Stamatis, Chris Eskew, Brent Lucy, Graham Thompson, Zeynep Aksöz
Design Team KOKKUGIA: Roland Snooks, Pablo Kohan, Fleet Hower
Client: Yeosu 2012 Expo Committee

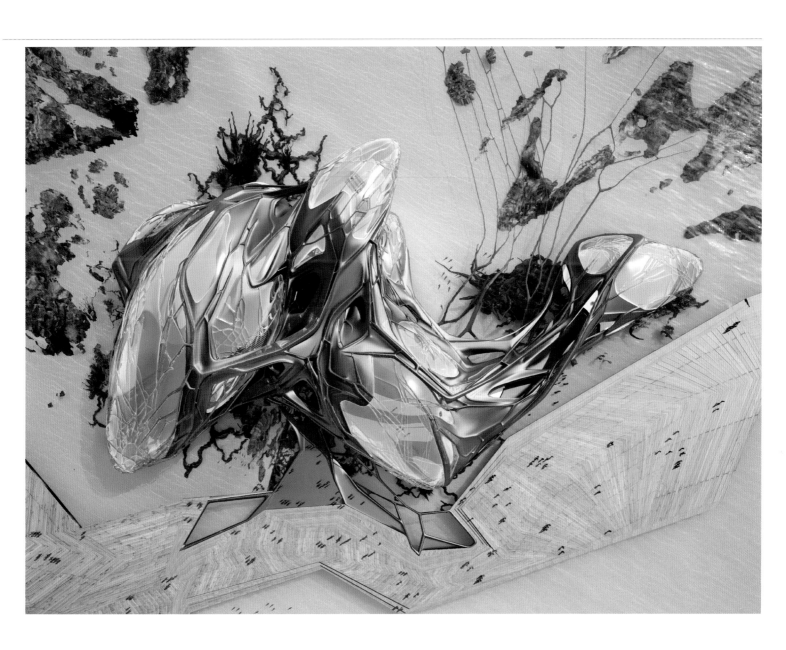

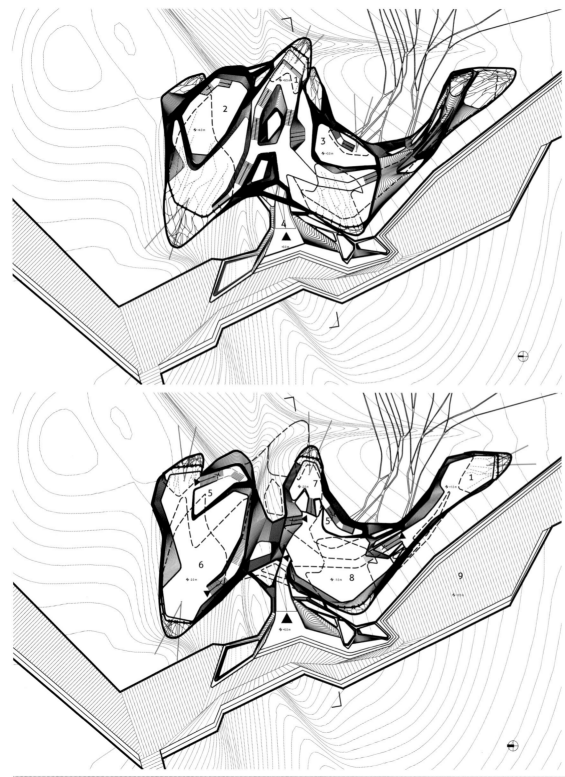

1. Ocean view gallery
2. Sea anemone exhibition
3. Jellyfish exhibition
4. Entrance
5. Support
6. Marine culture exhibition
7. Underwater gallery
8. Marine technology exhibition
9. Promenade

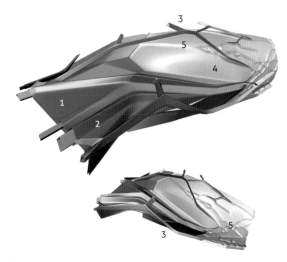

Structural diagram

1. Fiber composite shell
2. Structural pleats
3. Mohawks: Stabilizing armatures for
   ETFE membrane
4. ETFE membrane
5. Air beams: pressurized double
   pleats in membrane

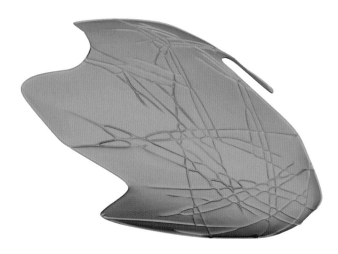

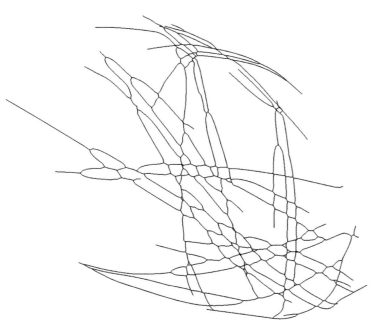

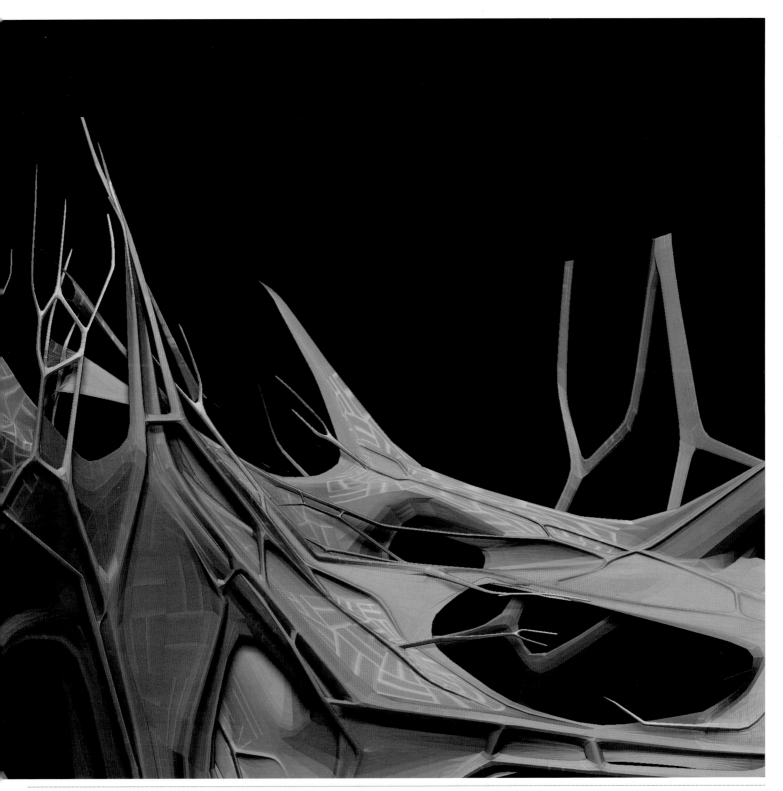

Tom Wiscombe Design
ARTIC Mass-Painting

This proposal is based on creating a complex visual oscillation between two and three dimensional realms. Somewhere between the disciplines of sculpture and painting, the piece registers as a mass but also as a graphic. Loopy, spotted patterns flow over manifold surfaces, simultaneously dissolving the mass and re-establishing it. Transparent zones allow people to view deep inside the object, their gaze pulled into involutions in interior surfaces. They can see the inside of the mass-painting.

The human brain, recent neuroscience suggests, is not engaged in "seeing" space, but in actively "modelling" space[1]. Residing on multiple ontological levels, this project is an attempt to force the brain to hedge and guess in its "modelling" of physical reality.

The colorful pattern language, while fanciful at first glance, is not simply a visual phenomenon. It is the result of intersecting a map of structural stresses with a painterly sensibility. The loopy mass is analyzed as a composite shell structure, revealing areas of low and high stress. The resultant color-gradient map is transferred to a digital paint environment where it is manipulated to produce certain visual effects but also broken down into layers of variable thickness and material strength. Color and pattern therefore only partially index material forces; the piece exceeds simple material expression towards something which correlates nature and culture. Finally, layers of super-thin technology are embedded into the structurally sedimented fiber composite shell. Thin film solar tape is tucked beneath the outermost layer of the shell, while organic-LED lighting film is embedded on the inside, in light-colored layers. The solar tape creates micro-patterning which breaks down large surfaces and generates energy to power the lighting of the piece. At night, the lighting creates mysterious graphic and silhouette effects, heightening the dimensional play of the piece.

1. Alessio Erioli, Lecture, Intensive Aesthetics, Innsbruck, June 17, 2011.

Design team: Tom Wiscombe, Robbie Eleazer, Mitch Rocheleau, Mo Harmon
Art consultant: Rebecca O'Leary
Client: City of Anaheim Public Works Director
Location: Anaheim, 2011

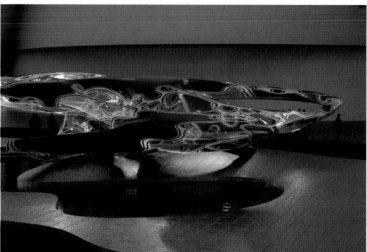

1. **Solar tape:** Strips of solar tape embedded under a layer of e-glass.

2. **Dyed fiber composite:** Three to five layers of variably colored glass fiber weave.

3. **Clear acrylic membrane:** Acrylic shell localized in areas of minimal structural stress.

4. **OLED:** Organic light-emitting diode below fiber composite strips of solar tape.

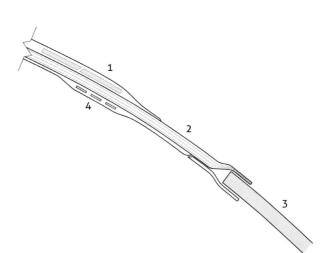

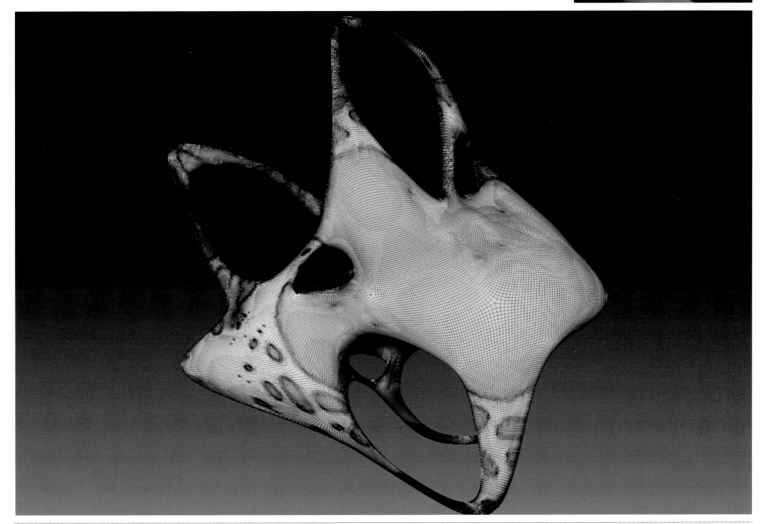

Tom Wiscombe Design

Beijing National Hotel

At 1,500 rooms, this hotel will be the largest hotel in Beijing. It is located near the Beijing International Airport in the 5th Ring, and will be used to host international conferences. The building is 303 meters long and is intended to become a major landmark, visible to landing aircraft.

The building is organized around three volumetric rings fused together by surfaces draped from the top and bottom. The rings create atriums which are enclosed by ETFE domes, housing a 10,000 sqm (32,808 sqft) interior rainforest as well as the conference center and hotel amenities. Rooms, radiating out along each ring, are oriented both outwards and inwards, creating views out to the city as well as down into the rainforest. The droop of the rings towards the perimeter of the building also allows views outward from the interiors of the rings. Structural bays are flexible and can be broken down into standard, business suite, and presidential types. A sky restaurant is located at the highest level of the building, with views out to the city in all directions.

The enclosure of the building is a double skin system where the outer layer is a weather break and the inner layer is the weatherproof enclosure. This creates a thermal buffer zone as well as the freedom to design a freeform pattern of apertures unrelated to the relentless horizontality of the hotel floor plates. The outer skin is supported by a lightweight cable-net structure which is stabilized by large tension rings affixed at the top and perimeter of the building.

The skin is also embedded with a second system of solar thermal pipes and grey water capture grooves which hybridizes the base diamond pattern with a sporadic weaving pattern. Driven by Tom Wiscombe's long-time interest in complex biological systems, structure, skin, and thermal systems are interwoven in such a way that they cannot be reduced back to their parts.

Design principal: Tom Wiscombe
Location: Beijing, China

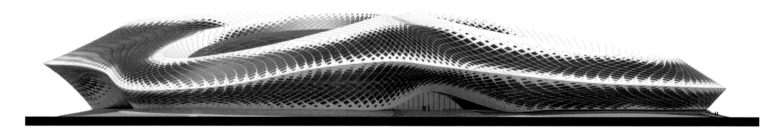

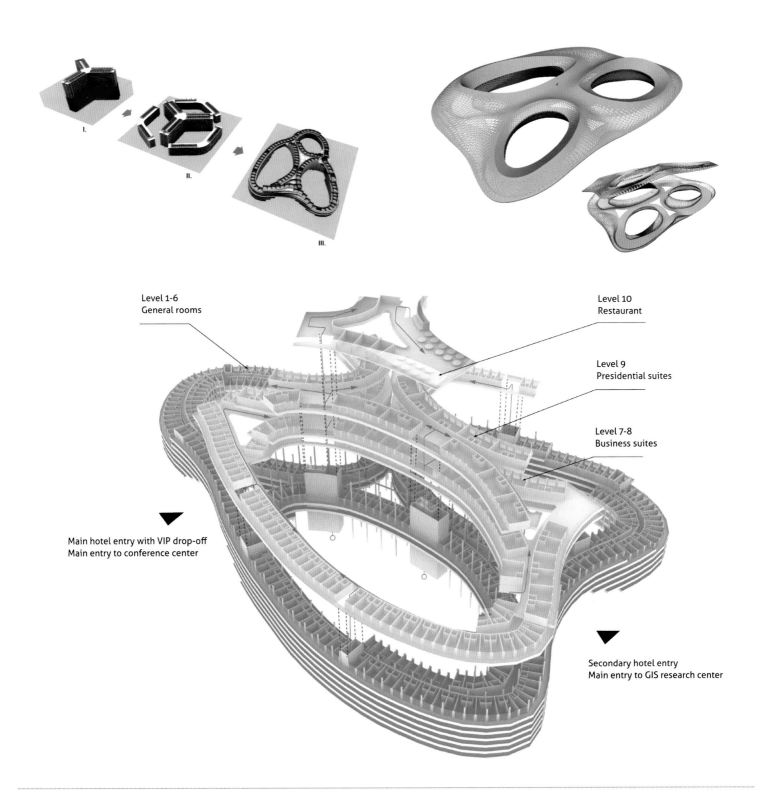

I.

II.

III.

Level 1-6
General rooms

Level 10
Restaurant

Level 9
Presidential suites

Level 7-8
Business suites

Main hotel entry with VIP drop-off
Main entry to conference center

Secondary hotel entry
Main entry to GIS research center

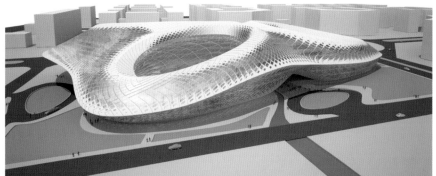

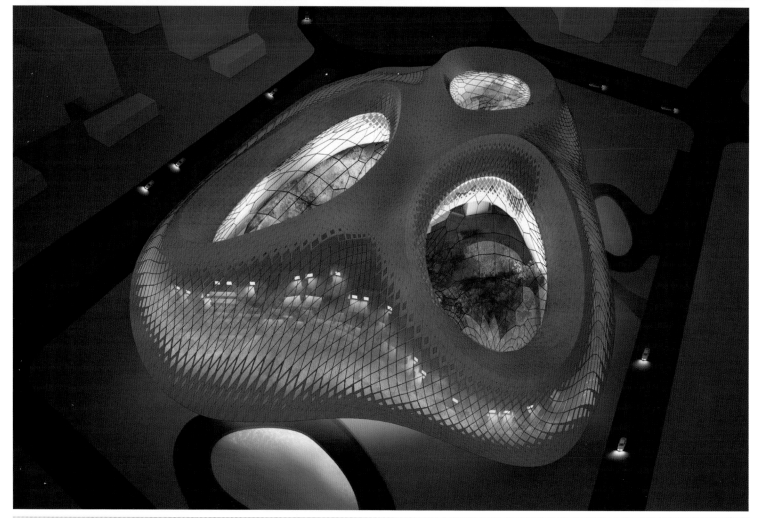

Pattern of solar thermal water and chilled ceiling

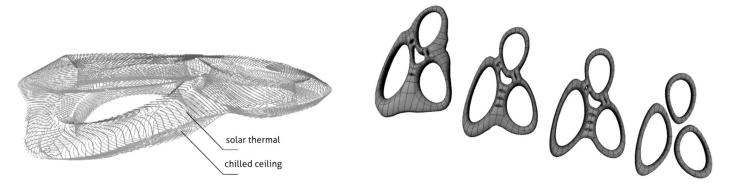

solar thermal

chilled ceiling

Structure diagram

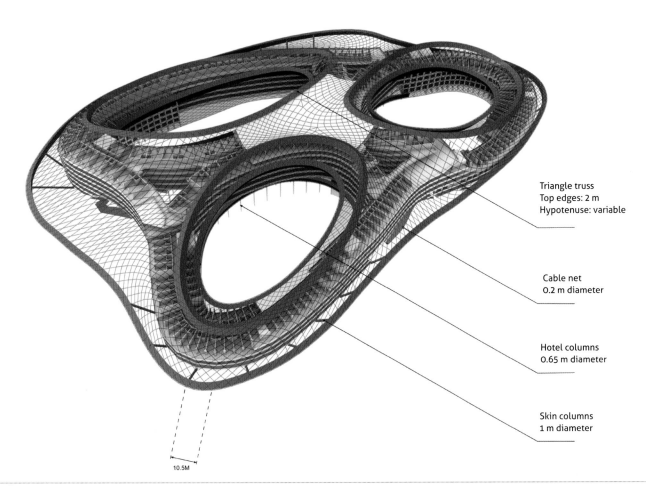

Triangle truss
Top edges: 2 m
Hypotenuse: variable

Cable net
0.2 m diameter

Hotel columns
0.65 m diameter

Skin columns
1 m diameter

10.5M

Tom Wiscombe Design
Busan Opera House

This opera is a synthetic mountain. It stands in stark contrast to the horizontality of the Marine Culture District, and relates to the mountainous topography that bounds and characterizes the city. It can be seen from all over the bay as a strong silhouette.

The mountain contains two nested volumes which house the 2000 seat Opera and the 1300 seat Multifunctional Theater. The outer shell of the mountain loosely contains these volumes, sometimes fusing with them, sometimes vaulting over them, and sometimes dissolving away to create views and passageways through. Openings in the mountain are positioned towards views of the city and the waterfront.

The manifold skin of the mountain varies from razor-thin and roof-like to extremely thick and spatial, where it is packed with public amenities and private support functions. Elevator cores and other circulation elements also inhabit these poché spaces rather than being expressed. The double-layer mass is therefore an organizational device rather than simply a formal expression.

The cavernous space inside the mountain operates as a microclimate. It is outdoors but feels enclosed; the 'roof' and 'walls' of the outer shell create spatial boundary, but also act as a sun shade and wind and rain break. The extreme environmental conditions of Busan's hot summer days and monsoon rains are mediated to create a comfortable, protected urban space all year long.

The mountain sits on top of a plinth. The plinth is not fused with the mountain in order to retain the independence of ground and building-object. It houses support functions such as parking, delivery, staging, storage, and technical rooms.

Design team: Tom Wiscombe, David Stamatis, Robbie Eleazer, Mitch Rocheleau, Fernando Herrera, Jason Orbe-Smith, Cindy Lin, Klarke Wang
Location: Busan, S. Korea

The figural apertures in the mountain create deep space, drawing in visitors, and creating high-contrast lighting situations. An intricate pattern of architectural tracery weaves these deep apertures together with a system of windows, or penetrations in the manifold. The effect is one of mysterious irresolution between deep mass and super-flatness.

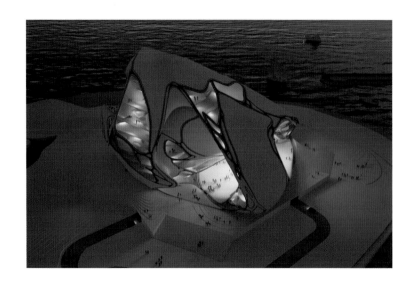

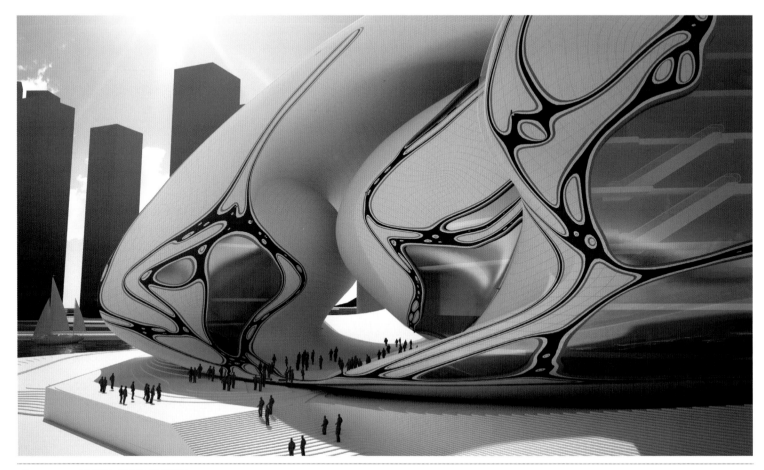

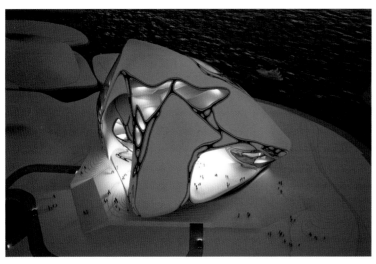

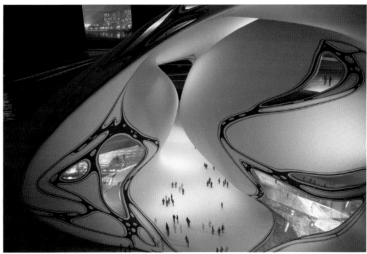

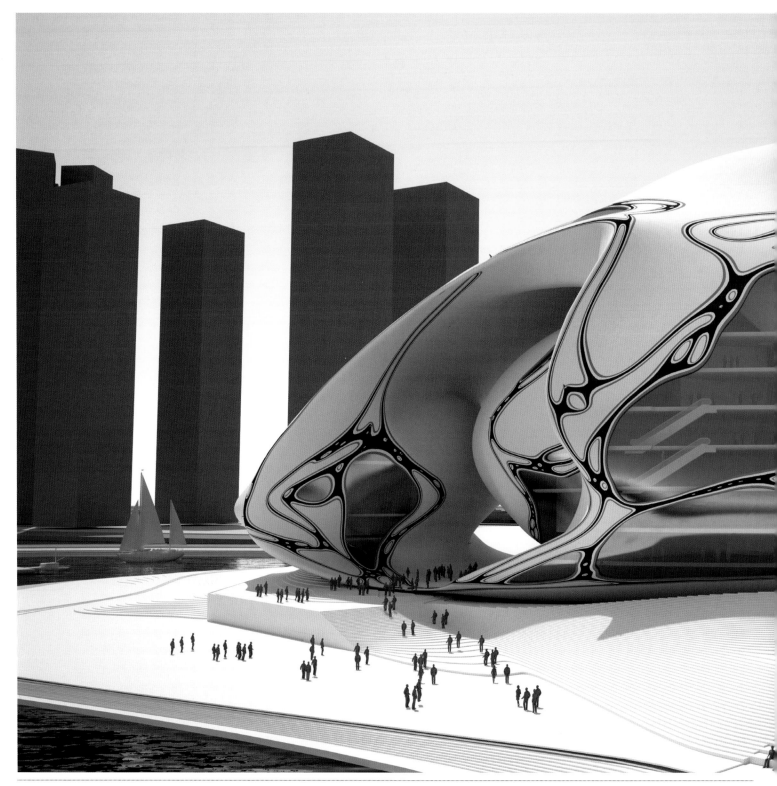

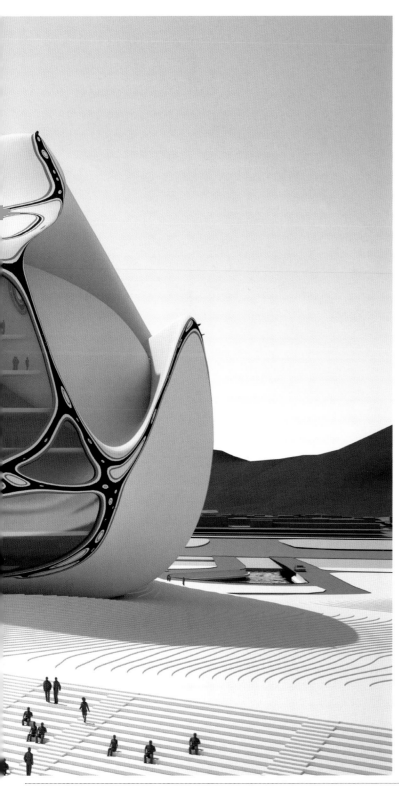

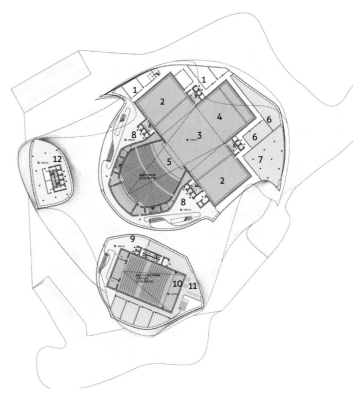

1. Office
2. Side stage
3. Main stage
4. Back stage
5. Orchestra
6. Storage
7. Conference room
8. Mezzanine
9. Foyer
10. Stage
11. Performers' lounge
12. Shopping

1. Stress map of base shape.

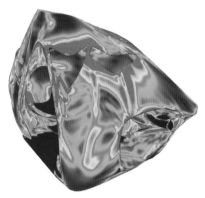

2. Variable stresses appear when apertures are introduced.

3. Structural Tattoos generated based on structural information and painterly sensibility.

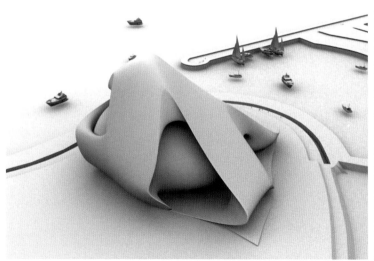

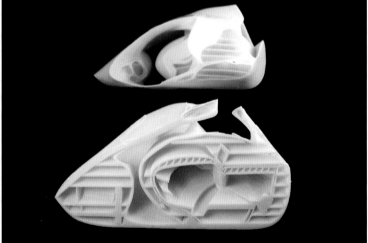

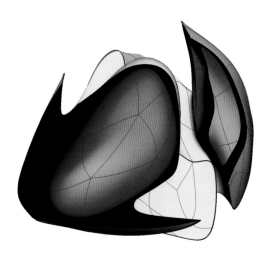

The cavernous space inside the mountain creates a microclimate. It is outdoor but feels enclosed; the 'roof' and 'walls' of the outer shell create spatial boundary, but also act as a sun shade and wind and rain break. The extreme environmental conditions of Busan's hot summer days and monsoon rains are mediated to create a comfortable, protected urban space all year long.

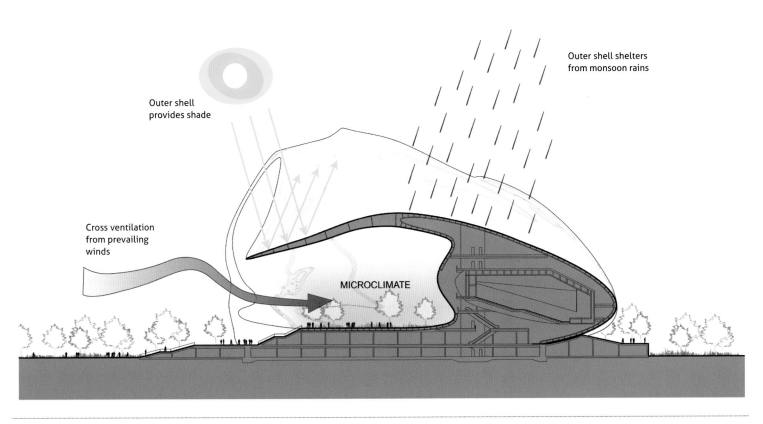

Outer shell provides shade

Outer shell shelters from monsoon rains

Cross ventilation from prevailing winds

MICROCLIMATE

Dave Eaton, Geoffrey Klein, Michael Wetmore
Living Bridge

The objective in designing Living Bridge was to describe a new type of nonlinear architecture through the design of an inhabitable bridge in Tokyo. The chosen site integrates with the residential neighborhoods of Ginza and Tsukishima. Through the harnessing and intensification of the discrete flows of the two neighborhoods, and through algorithmic generation of turbulent spatial and programmatic structures, a reinvention of the inhabitable bridge type is achieved.

Creating Living Bridge was a three-step process. Using Processing, the designers identified the movement patterns of people and vehicles in the city, considered them as agent-based systems of entangled flows, and modeled their interactions as a vector field. Next, they released decking agents to read the vector field, moving through it and creating walking, cycling, and vehicular paths. Finally, they introduced self-organizing components that changed their shape and connectivity depending on the turbulence of the field. The components thereby simultaneously create, channel, and enclose the interactions of the circulation and programs inhabiting the bridge, leading to a dynamic space that connects and activates the riverfront.

Agents are typed as pedestrian, bicycle and automobile in order to create paths that will be appropriate to their real life counterparts. The agents monitor their immediate area (blue cones in the diagram) and use the information they gather to modify their behavior (shifting their velocity from the white to the blue arrow in the diagram). Agents are attracted to city connections within their cone of vision. Depending on approach angle and agent type, each agent will decide whether to follow nearby vectors or avoid them. Some type-specific behaviors include general avoidance between automobiles and pedestrians as well as bi-directional flow for automobiles to maintain a major city artery.

An asymmetrical, Y-shaped component was chosen for its flexibility. Initially, components are placed near the edge of the area containing the vector field. Upon initial placement, each component aligns its long axis with the local vector field. In more turbulent areas, the component becomes flatter and less spindly to create enclosure for the program that will exist in those areas. Each arm of the component looks for other nearby components with the proper orientation for a connection. If it is within the distance and angle range, the arm rotates and extends to connect to its neighbor. Each long arm can accept up to four connections, while the short arm can only accept one. In a post process, the components are smoothed to create a flowing form.

Design: Dave Eaton, Geoffrey Klein, Michael Wetmore
Teachers: Cecil Balmond, Roland Snooks - University of Pennsylvania, School of Design

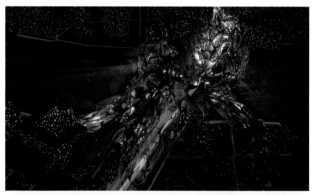

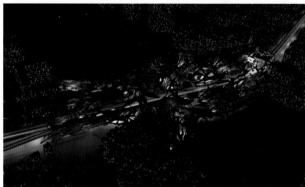

The objective in designing Living Bridge was to describe a new type of nonlinear architecture through the design of an inhabitable bridge in Tokyo. The chosen site integrates with the residential neighborhoods of Ginza and Tsukishima. Through the harnessing and intensification of the discrete flows of the two neighborhoods, and through algorithmic generation of turbulent spatial and programmatic structures, a reinvention of the inhabitable bridge type is achieved.

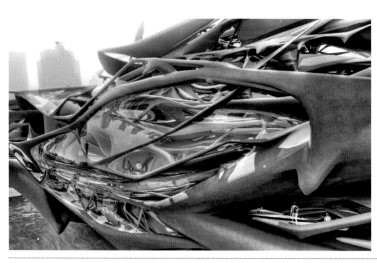

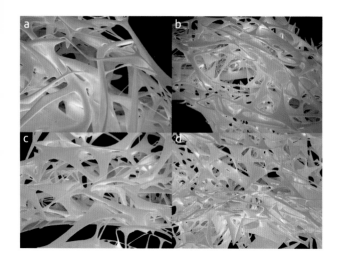

The vector field smoothly transitions between linear and turbulent qualities, expressed through component variations. Areas of turbulence are characterized by enveloping enclosure ideal for programmed space, while areas of linearity are ideal for transitory space.

a. Transitional (detail)
b. Turbulent
c. Linear
d. Transitional

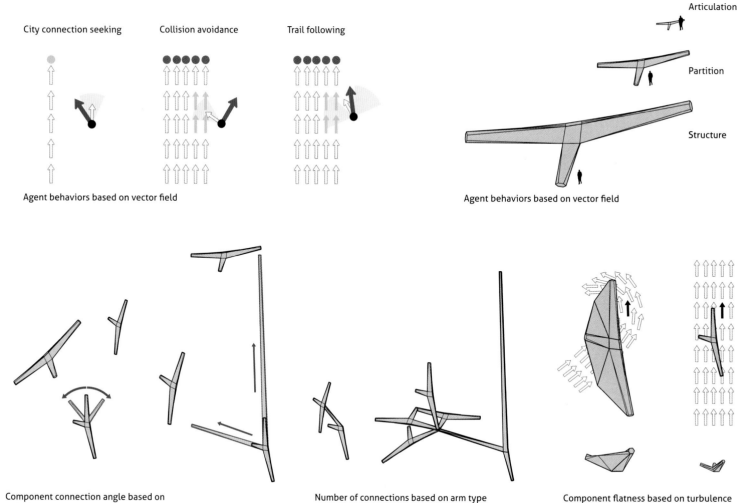

City connection seeking

Collision avoidance

Trail following

Agent behaviors based on vector field

Articulation

Partition

Structure

Agent behaviors based on vector field

Component connection angle based on neighbors

Number of connections based on arm type

Component flatness based on turbulence

Gage / Clemenceau Architects

Estonian Academy of the Arts

The façades, apertures, and large courtyard manifold openings of this project were designed using the software package Alias Studio, which is typically used for automotive design. By creating an experimental alliance with the software manufacturer, Autodesk, the designers misused the software with the express purpose of cross-pollinating automotive and architectural design tactics in the service of new directions and technologies for design and fabrication. Instead of relying on platonic geometries which typically guide architectural design decisions, the facade of the Estonian Academy of the Arts is entirely, and tautly, wrapped in what the automotive industry refers to as "Class-A" surfaces—surfaces which produce the maximum aesthetic effect with a minimum of mathematical description.

The building contains both purely aesthetic fluid ripples and contours, as well as performative scoops, tunnels and vents that funnel fresh air to all areas of the building—from the lobby to the interior courtyard, to the 5th floor central manifold featured in the center of the overall composition.

A large-scale prototype panel was constructed of the centralized section of the building in order to view these surface-based geometries at a larger, architectural scale.

To be more specific, automotive design is largely based on the placement of "break lines,"— the folds in panels which reach along the side of a car from the front to the back. The portion of the panel above the break line reflects the sky; the portion below it reflects the road. Careful curation of the break lines, therefore, allows car designers to capitalize on the relation between the viewer, the object, the ground and the sky— which is a problem normally specific to architecture, and generally solved through massing.

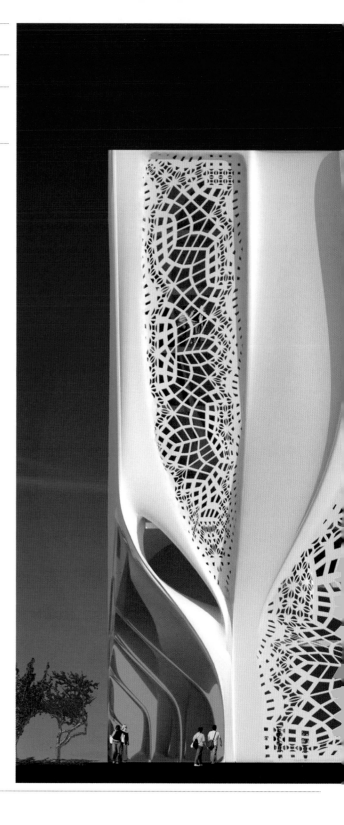

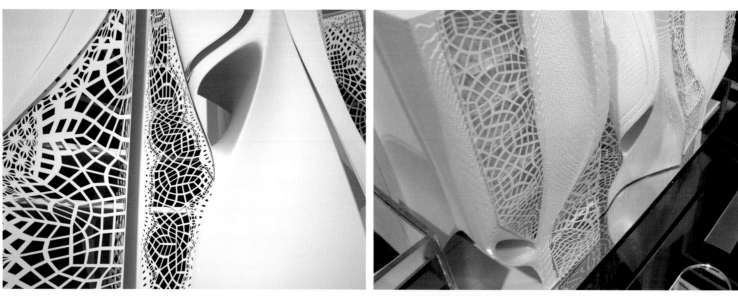

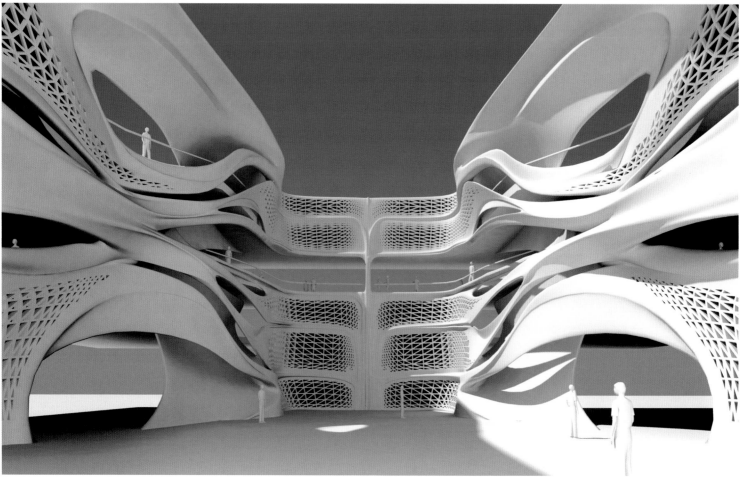

DIGITAL FORM-FINDING

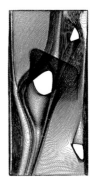
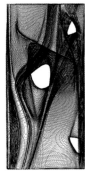
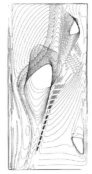
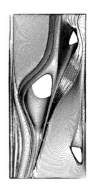
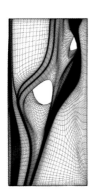

Minimaforms

Brunel Gateway

Through an invitation from world renowned performance artist Stelarc, Minimaforms was asked to develop a gateway structure for Brunel University. The pavilion structure is one of a family of architectural interventions that are proposed as part of a university campus works project. The brief was to develop a system that would correlate these interventions and identify critical sites as a means to restructure the public space of a university that has expanded rapidly in recent years beyond its original campus design. Brunel Gateway is a seeing machine, structured as an open-cell network that operates through a series of operable convex and concave lenses, amplifying and collapsing the experiential relationships between users and their context. Developed through a parametrically controlled cellular deployment system, these lenses are distributed with both optical and structural parameters at play. The underbellies of these lenses extend as part of a three-dimensional fiber field in which structural fibers and optic hairs are set out. The access plane hovering over the water surface of the reflection pool is constructed as a series of walkable lily pads that enable users to experience a complete sensorial displacement as they move through this architecture of interface.

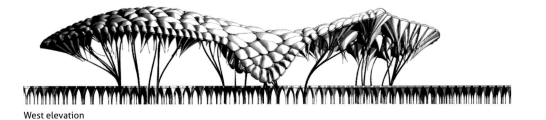

West elevation

South elevation

DIGITAL FORM-FINDING

East elevation

North elevation

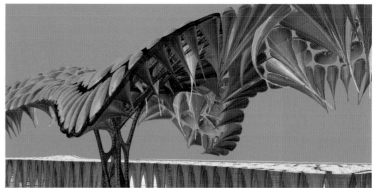
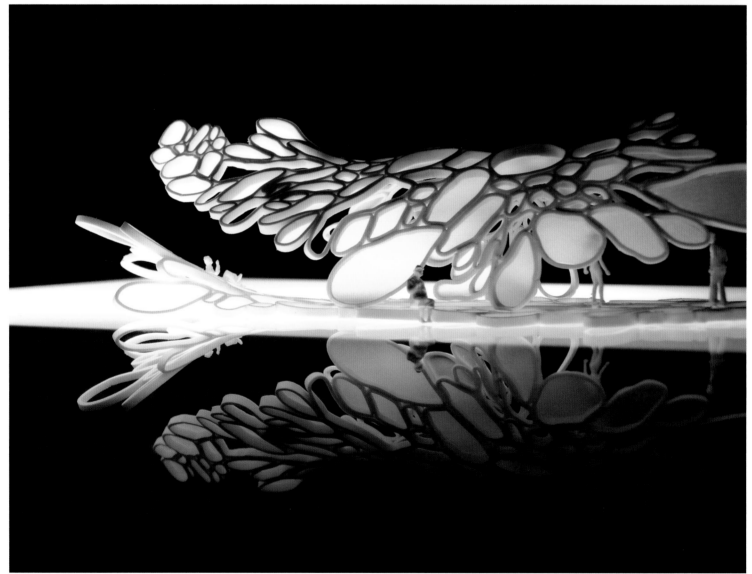

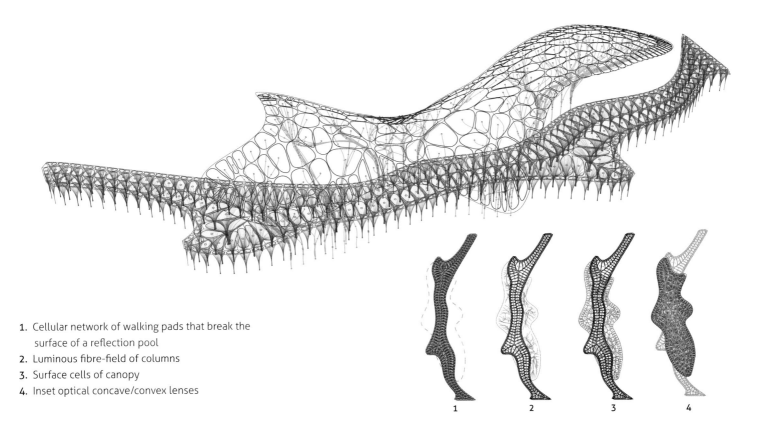

1. Cellular network of walking pads that break the surface of a reflection pool
2. Luminous fibre-field of columns
3. Surface cells of canopy
4. Inset optical concave/convex lenses

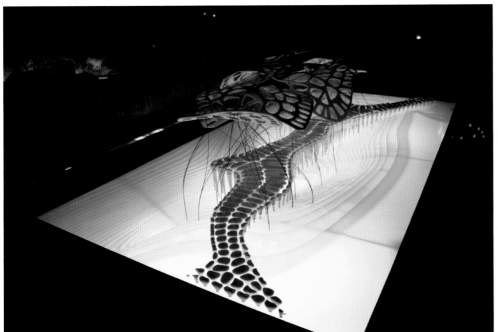

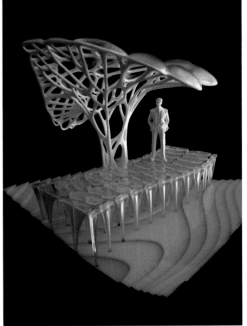

Arphenotype

Anthropometric Pavilion

The Anthropometric Pavilion (Anthropomorphic = of human shape) develops its form language from the symbiosis of the Modulor developed by Le Corbusier combined with the Moebius strip (by Johann Benedict Listing and August Ferdinand Möbius). The Modulor understood itself as bridging the imperial and metric systems; the idea is bound up with the "Möbiusband" as an endless Feedback Loop. In this way, the pavilion creates a harmonizing bridge between Germany and India. Le Corbusier himself stands for an early co-operation between Germany/Europe and India.

One special feature is the color of the Pavilion, which is realized by an LED net mounted on the membrane. The LED net illuminates moving pictures with the colors of the Indian and German national flags, thus taking up and visually integrating the idea of the "Infinite Opportunities" logo into the design.

The Moebius strip divides the Pavilion into two central amorphous regions; the main area with stage, auditorium, bar and a small kitchen, and the second area which is the "modifiable area". This serves as an "open air" stage, or if necessary, it can be divided into small information booths for different agencies. Both areas are separately accessible, so that a distinct operational sequence of meetings would be possible.

Since it is not yet clear exactly where the Pavilion will be constructed, an organic sketch was consciously selected, which can react to different urban scenarios. It also supplements the flow and transition between interior and exterior space via terraces.

Pipes, which are bent by CNC technology, form the basis of the construction. The second layer consists of membranes, which are stretched between the pipes. By creating a larger distance between the pipes, the membranes themselves will "stretch into form" and create a rigid horizontal structure. "The membranes draw the Design in Form". The construction process is similar to a tent structure and can be realized without mechanical help. Another advantage is the minimal storage for the dismantled structure, which also leads to easier transport.

Collaborators:
designtoproduction, Arnold Walz
Dr. Victor Wilhelm
Buro Happold, Dr. Shrikant Sharma
Lightlife, Antonius Quodt
Lavingia Consultants, Raj Lavingia

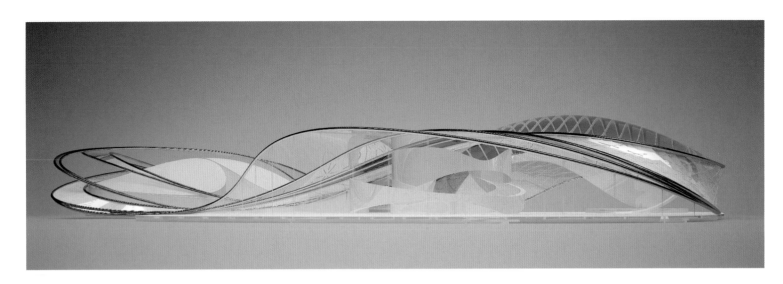

1. Mobile toilet system
2. Small conference rooms
3. Kitchen, backstage, storage
4. Stage
5. Large space, film projections
6. Bar
7. Terrace
8. Foundation
9. CNC bending
10. Transparent membrane
11. Translucent membrane

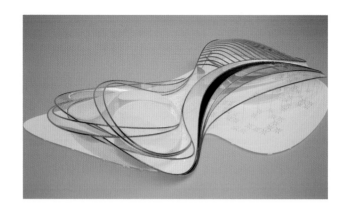

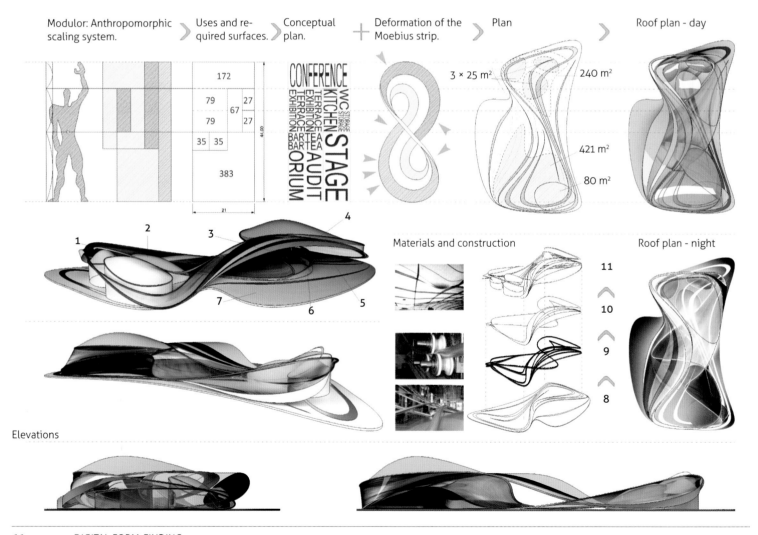

Modulor: Anthropomorphic scaling system.

Uses and required surfaces.

Conceptual plan.

Deformation of the Moebius strip.

Plan

3 × 25 m² 240 m²

421 m²

80 m²

Roof plan - day

CONFERENCE
KITCHEN STAGE
WC STAGE
STORAGE
EXHIBITION
TERRACE
EXHIBITION
TERRACE
BARTEA
BARTEA
ORIUM
AUDIT

Materials and construction

11
10
9
8

Roof plan - night

Elevations

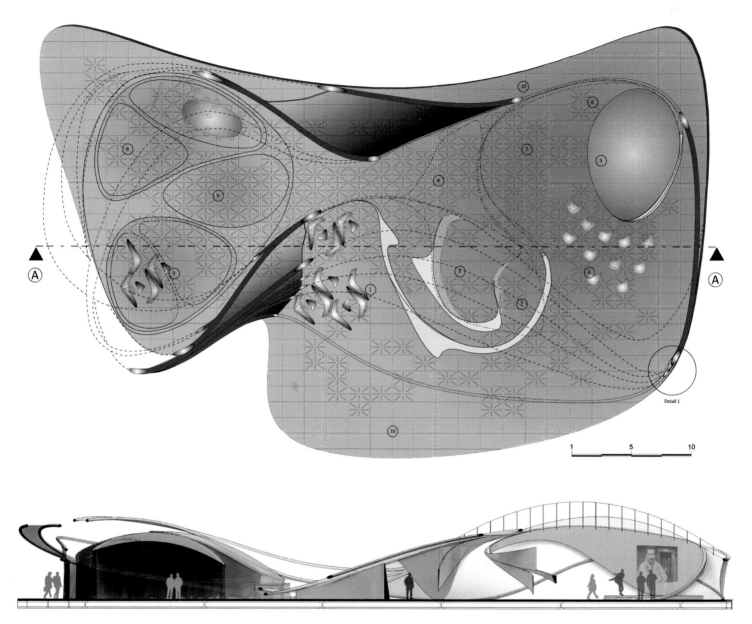

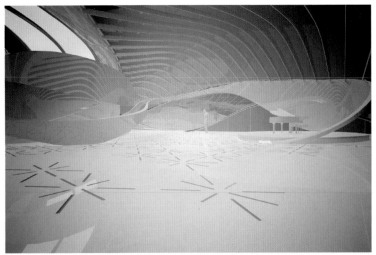

The pavilion is, through the use of innovative materials, up to 99% recyclable. The modern developed membranes are compostable; the foundation is built of concrete. The pipes are designed in aluminium, which can be later reused. Only the technical equipment would need to be disposed of.

Arphenotype

Fractal Transformations

Fractal Transformations deals with the blurring of different software modelling / generating techniques and scripted fractal generators into a spider net-like sculpture. The object functions as a visual stimulator for a poetic reaction in the human mind; it generates space like a toxic cell, while the human feels displaced in space, not location. Shadows and light generate a surreal gap; the skin mimics artificial porcelain with its subsurface scattering effect. The distinction between the object and the human as performer blur, while in real-time the reflections of the surrounding glass walls are hard and sharp.

This work asks a number of philosophical questions. Where is the seduction in air? Is Lucy Irigaray still fighting the war of the genders? Where is Heidegger now? In there? The blood of the enlightened is white like a flashlight in a storm, like a golden ear, van Gogh cut a nice sphere. We are here, what else is there?

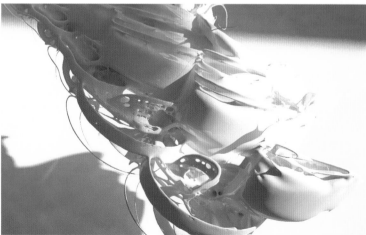

Joseph A. Sarafian

Emergent Porosity

This project imagines a future in which billions of genetic algorithms act not only as the mediator between man and reality, but shape his existence through their very interactions. It explores a functionality beyond the carrying out of human desires, of the prediction of human behavior. These ideas manifest in the design of the Bach Multidisciplinary Research Institute. Derived from notions of how Johann Sebastian Bach wove together voices in his fugues, this design is a synthesis of various flows of information, creating an effect larger than the sum of its parts. To achieve this goal, the building acts as an organism, reacting to its environment in such a way that it automatically controls its porosity through a network of advanced algorithms. Thus the façade is a continually fluctuating network of openings.

Instead of merely controlling the light conditions of the interiors, the aperture system is designed to close off and filter pollution from the adjacent freeway as part of the research of the facility. Thus by engaging with its environment the building acts as a testing instrument as much as an enclosure. Acoustical considerations are addressed on a local level as spaces that require varying levels of insulation are opened or closed automatically and in relation to human occupancy.

Flanked by Grand Avenue and an off-ramp of the 101 Freeway in Downtown Los Angeles, this site poses a unique set of challenges. Noise and car pollution are controlled through the pyramidal apertures that can close off sound, light, air, or all three depending on which layer of the double skin system is closed. This building envelope is comprised of carbon-fiber panels that enclose a shell of glass apertures. The glass is actually an assembly of two thin glass sheets with a membrane of translucent Aerogel insulation that adds to its acoustical and thermal insulation abilities. This enclosure system functions as the mediator between interior and exterior, and is controlled by an individual, agent based system. Each occupant has his own algorithm of light preferences and thus controls the system locally, contributing to the movement of the array as a whole when the needs of many are seen acting as an amalgamation.

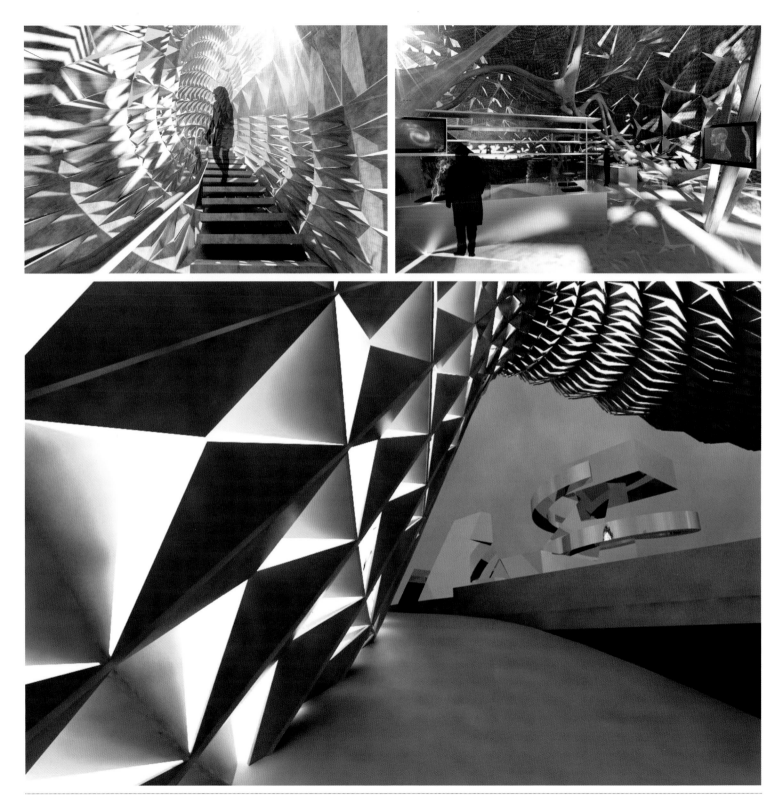

The research institute is designed to engage various fields of study, from music and the visual arts to biology and mathematics. This diversity promotes a common wealth of knowledge and facilitates interdisciplinary learning. Advancements in one field will have ripple effects in others and this synergy will promote a culture of recombinatory knowledge.

The building form and structure is generated by an agent-based flocking algorithm in which agents from various locations on the site create paths following those of structural loads, determining the location of primary and secondary structural members.

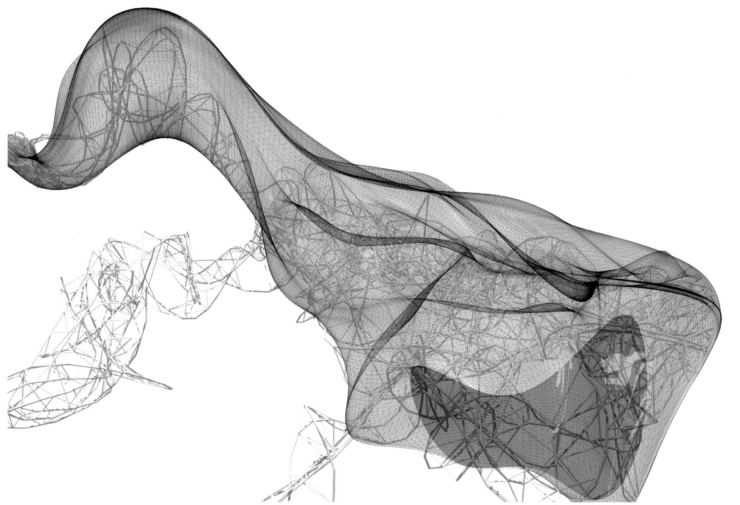

moh architects

Birnbeck Pier

The site conjures the common architectural dilemma of how to achieve simultaneity of two typically exclusive spatial qualities: an iconic figure and open space. On the one hand, Birnbeck Island represents a pivotal point within the distinctive identity and picturesque promenade along North Somerset seafront. As such, it seems perfectly fitting for a figural landmark and it may well be argued that such an iconic development would have an important regeneration effect both locally as well as regionally.

On the other hand, however, any large aggregation of built space would inevitably erode the pier's principal spatial qualities: blocking as yet unobstructed vistas towards mainland and sea, obstructing lively open plazas for promenading, leisure and public gathering and so on and so forth. Moreover, any 'icon' in the traditional sense of a monumental building would pose a disproportionate counterweight to both the existing historic fabric as well as the delicate natural backdrop.

The designers' main ambition is to overcome the aforementioned dichotomy and suggest a model that acknowledges the necessity for an icon in order to foster the attractiveness of the region, and yet responds to the existing spatial qualities, the historic fabric and the subsequent size constraints. In order to achieve this, they propose a spatial formation where the open space is modulated in such a way that it becomes the icon itself, rather than the built space in a traditional figure-ground composition.

As with most pier structures, the current layout of Birnbeck island suggests an almost mono-directional flow of visitors: While entering the site from the city, or likewise approaching from the far end of the pier, all access is bundled in between the existing buildings and the platform. Instead of sticking with this rather monotonous routing pattern the project's program distribution is generated from a circulation diagram that instead allows for multiple ways to experience the extraordinary site: The *flâneur* is presented with open vistas towards the sea, framed passages in between historic fabric and proposed project, tranquil plazas and raised platforms allowing for unobscured views over the entire island.

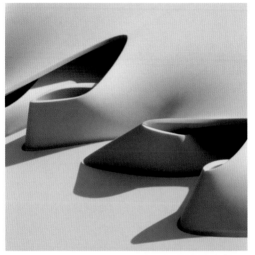

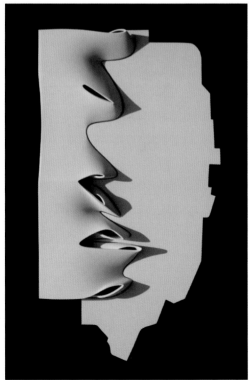

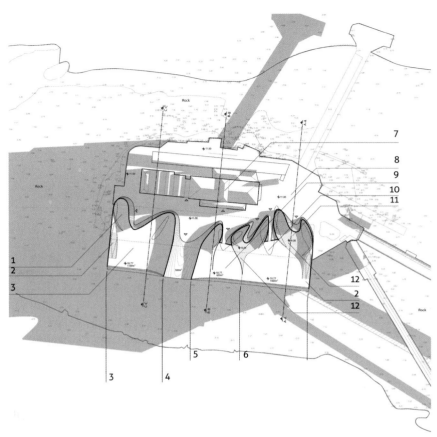

1. Polifunctional hall / entrance area
2. Service, bathrooms
3. Polifunctional hall for banquets, concerts, exhibitions, city council meetings
4. Outdoor plaza
5. Restaurant - cafe
6. Weston Super Mare Casino
7. Restaurants, souvenir shops, bars, cafes
8. Bell Tower Plaza
9. Cafe, bar, restaurant
10. Casino entrance area on pier deck level
11. Casino spaces on lower level
12. Poker, blackjack, roulete

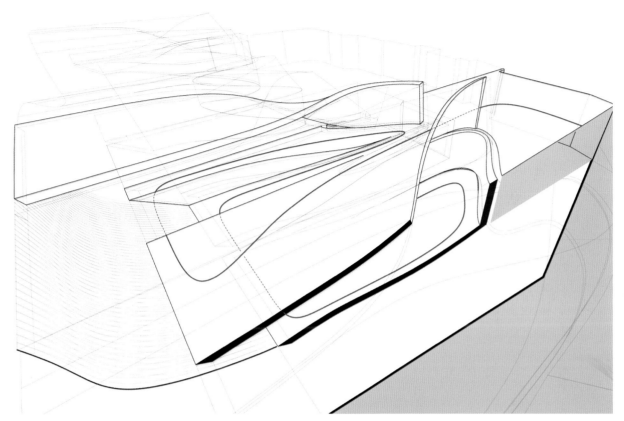

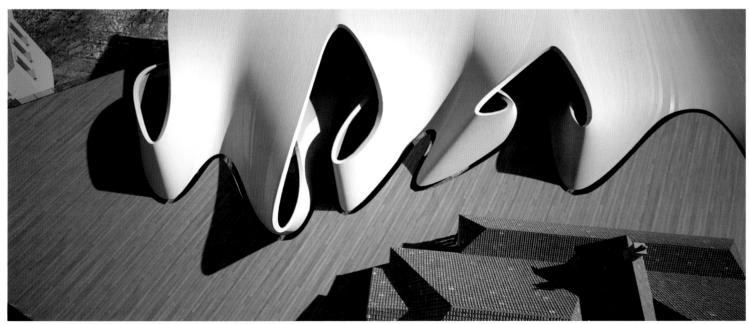

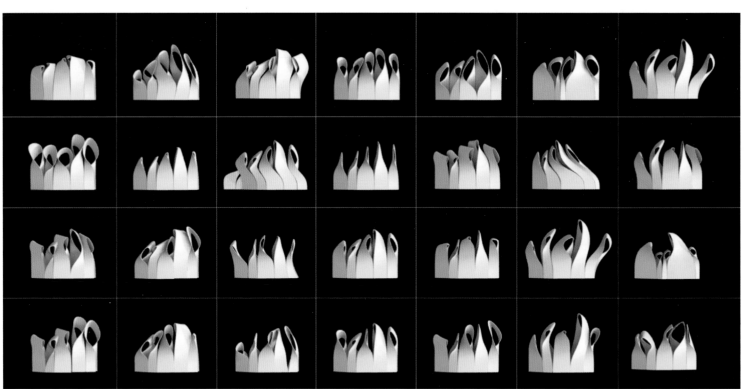

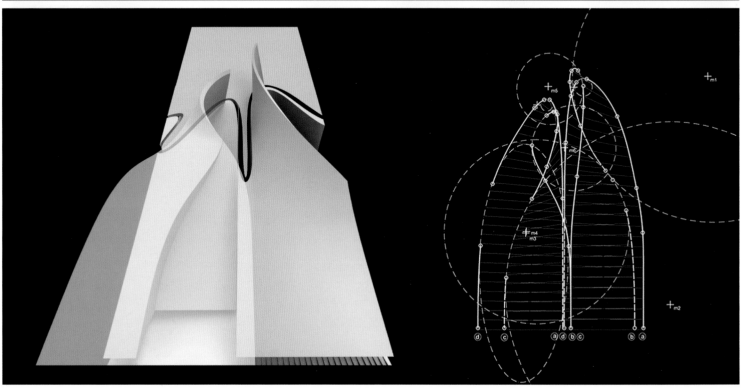

The routing diagram deliberately does not differentiate between inside and outside spaces per se, thus allowing for uninterrupted transitions between all appending spaces of the proposal in a continuous and fluid manner, be it inside or outside. Yet, should any part of the proposed program need to be temporarily cut off from the cohesive network (e.g. for private or semi-private uses), all access remains fully functional as the chosen pattern allows for dynamical re-routing.

Correspondingly, the program is distributed alongside these routes as one continuous surface, allowing for circulation over the entire roofed area - where it becomes a gently sloped topography - as well as through the appending interior programs where it forms façades and/or apertures. While its formally intricate articulation generates enough attraction to function as an 'icon' - and thus promotes a lively urban environment - the structure maintains a low profile across the entire section. It never antagonizes the existing buildings or overpowers the delicate natural backdrop.

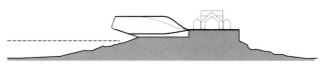

Section AA - Multifunctional hall

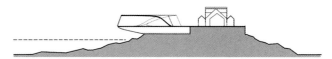

Section BB - Restaurant

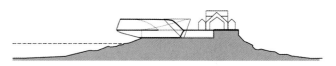

Section CC - Casino

Tobias Klein

Inverted Embodiment

Some of Klein's work has been centered on a fascination with the masterpiece of Sir Christopher Wren, St Paul's Cathedral. This is a place that, since the first service was held there in 1697, has celebrated, mourned and commemorated people and events of overwhelming importance to the country. Important services have included the funerals of Lord Nelson, the Duke of Wellington and Sir Winston Churchill; peace services marking the end of the First and Second World Wars; the launch of the Festival of Britain; the Service of Remembrance and Commemoration for the 11 September 2001; the 80th and 100th birthdays of Queen Elizabeth and the Queen Mother; and of course the wedding of Charles, Prince of Wales, to Lady Diana Spencer.

Although Klein's attempts to work with such an overwhelming building may seem irrational, highly speculative and not buildable, the work is not too dissimilar to the spirit and character of this great building itself. St Paul's has always undergone revolutionary changes of styles, for instance its trademark mosaic floor, which was later added as a result of Queen Victoria's mid-19th century complaint that the interior was 'most dreary, dingy and undevotional.' So, Klein argues, in the classical sense St Paul's might not reassemble what we call traditionally a building but is a true piece of architecture, a place for constant speculation, testing, and a monument to a true contested architecture.

In this spirit, these works cannot be read only as a geometric composition or a frivolous counterfeit of an embodied space, over-scaled and centered in what was the first ever constructed triple dome. The work needs to be read as a contextualized and tested speculative architecture, exploring the boundaries of a new embodied architecture that is articulated and situated within the cultural construct of St Paul's as one of the most extreme forms of ecclesial architecture.

Inverted Embodiment is the final piece in a series of three models build over 3 consecutive years. All models use complex voxel data constructs, derived by a magnetic resonance scanning of the designer's own body, generating the embodied qualities of the iconographic interiority of the triple dome. This finally completes the cycle of inversion and eversion thematic in the context of sacral and ecclesial architecture. It uses a 4-dimensional translation of space to articulate the last step of the inverted space as a fully embodied architectural argument. The reminiscent contextual elements bend away under a double-reflected space of the everted second dome of St Paul's.

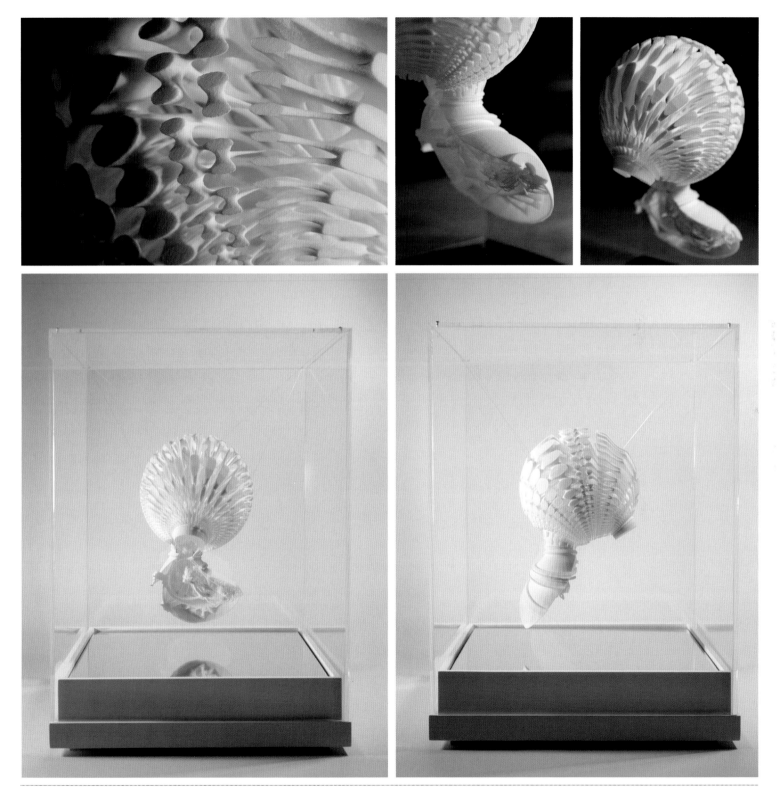

s[toggle]

Venom

How does one rethink an opera? There is no lack in ambition. But more often than not ambition becomes pretentious. The constant all-consuming urge for innovation can be destructive and self serving. But there is no mistaking the impact of creative processes fuelled by these seemingly undesirable traits. To dissect the traditional opera, gnawing away at the foundations of the sacred opera house till that threshold is reached when the hierarchies are disintegrated, when the instrument becomes the artist, and artist the facilitator.

The attempt was to transform the notion of a designed space into that of a designed intent. Performative spaces were achieved through articulations of the skin, the surface and the structure. Starting from a simple module, the articulations rise in complexity and hierarchy to sprout a new opera and concert hall in the middle of the Stadtpark in Vienna. The landscape is a manicured English garden which is transformed by the growth of the bionic music pavilion progressively mutating into an Opera. A relationship fluctuating between symbiotic and parasitic exists between the landscape and the opera in such a way that the boundaries are blurred. The interstitial spaces are colonized by a matrix of semi flexible biotic cell which undergoes mutation according to its specific situation. These cells exist in a state of flux between calcified structural cells, transparent circulation clusters, and lush botanical cells.

The opera is a music instrument that has a kaleidoscopic effect on the performances. The sound is selectively propagated into 4 quadrants based on the urban conditions. The opera is also an urban condenser, facilitating the streamlining of the multi modal flows surrounding Stadtpark. It creates new vistas and flow patterns and thus sculpts the urbanscape.

Studio: Studio Toggle
Design: Hend Almatrouk
Location: Vienna, Austria
Completion: June 2011

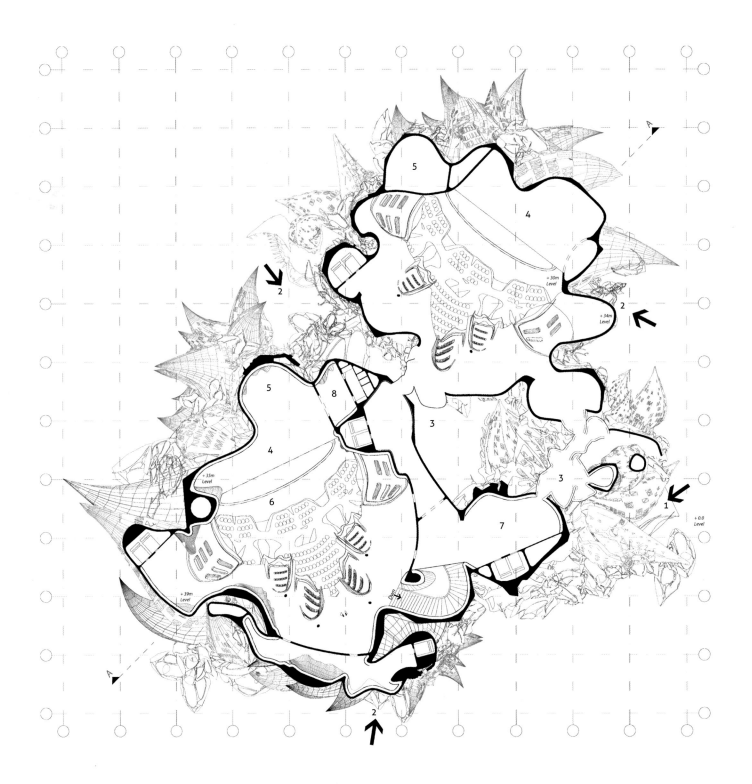

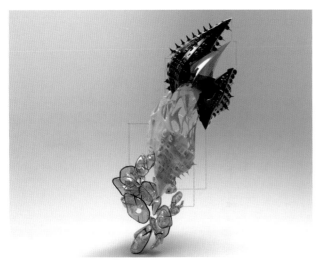

Assembly
1. Translucent plexiglass cells occupy the interstitial spaces.
2. Mettalic viscosity fuses with the structural cells
3. Viscous skin calcifies cracks and regenerates ceramic panels.
4. Moduled steel ribs forming the structure.

Plan
1. Main entrance
2. Entrance
3. Botanical garden
4. Stage
5. Backstage
6. Orchestra pit
7. Lobby and circulation
8. Rest room

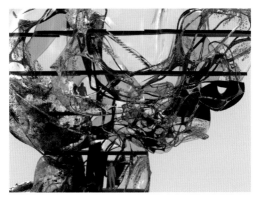
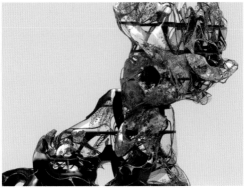

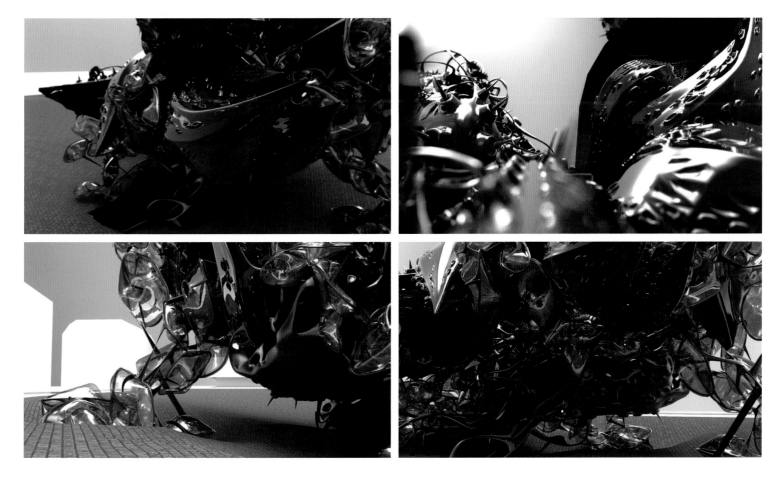

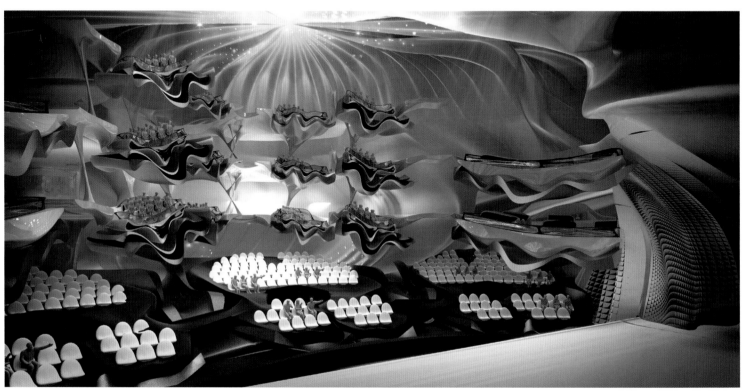

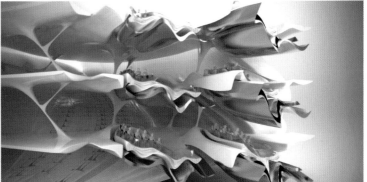

Studio Palermo

The Catasetum Project

This project is a design proposal for a Concert Hall at the Stadtpark in Vienna (Austria). Rethinking the concept of a Concert Hall the architectural emsemble of different geometrical and material configurations offers the opportunity for a multilayered and complex musical experience. The system includes central positioned classical, symmetric concert hall geometry, a further two areas created as sound shells in dependence on biological shell geometries (biomimicry) such as an ear or a mussle structure, and close to that a sound booth system of closed capsules for an intense and individual space for sound throughout the area. Other elements provide spaces and areas for a fully self-sufficient energy supply regarding ecological thinking, host interaction and active materials.

Rethinking the Concert Hall concept, introducing botanical gardens functioning as structure, evolving absolutistic symmetric building configurations into free floating geometry interdependencies, recombining system hierarchies with an adequate circulation organization, recombining the visitors attitude in it and the symbiotic form intergration to the surrounding park landscape are all contributing to the architectural qualities of the design.

Some key elements coming from Romanticism such as untamed wilderness, the unfinished and the validation of obscure perceptions. The Romantics were committed to the futility of comprehending the world with the aid of rational systems, as well as from the inferiority of every perfect thought compared to the inherent laws of nature. A New Romanticism approaches new areas in design and architecture processes - emerging aesthetic paradigms and systematic specifications.

Here is where the true transformation is happening. We are subverting the logic of perfection: what used to be about mastering the result of a non-perfect process is now about the production of monstrosity and the grotesque thought the mathematical perfection of an evolutive mechanism.

Design: Philip H. Wilck
Location: Vienna, Austria
Completion date: 2011

1. Viewing platform
2. Music experience center
3. Main Concert Hall
4. Stage equipment
5. Plenum
6. Technical support
7. Stage
8. Control room

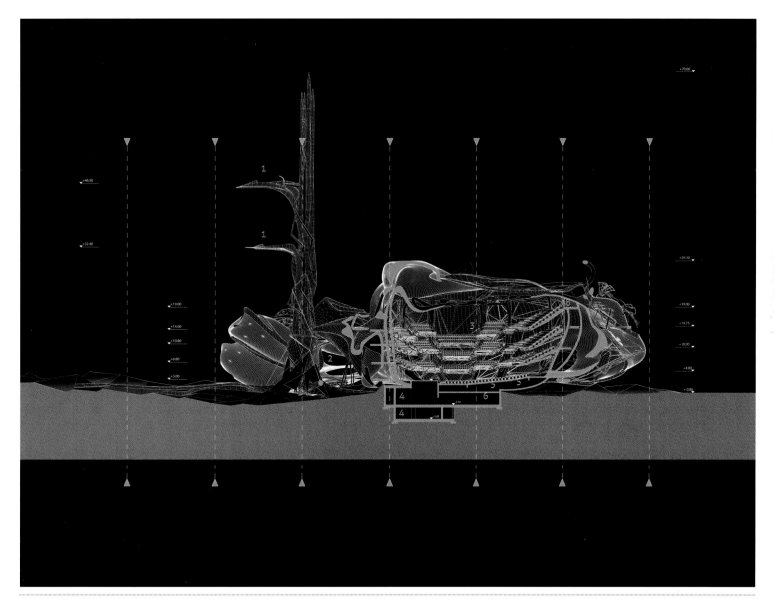

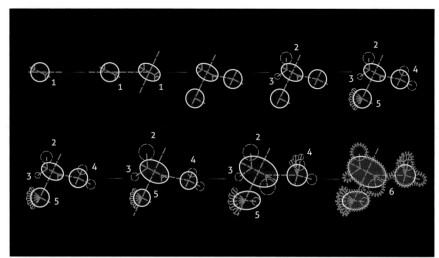

System Analysys

1. Parameter angle
2. Parameter distance
3. Parameter radius
4. Parameter position
5. Parameter multiplication
6. Enclosure system
7. Horizontal enclosure

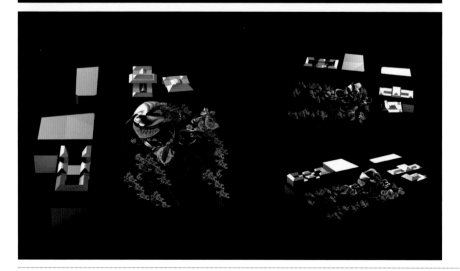

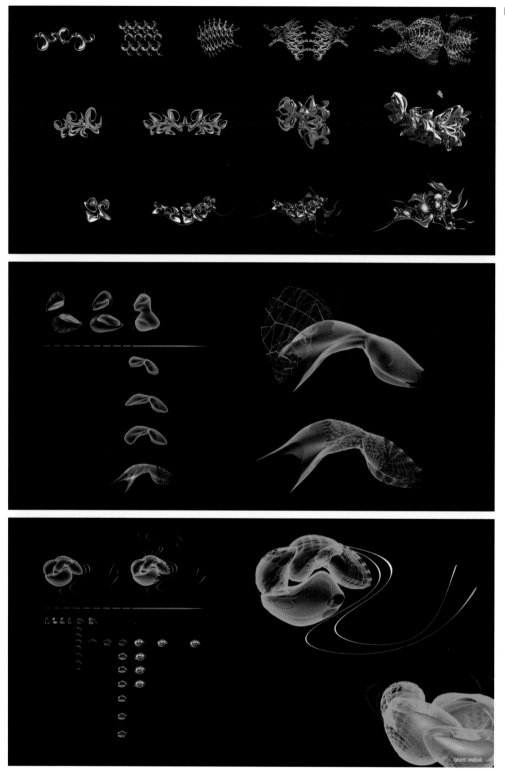

Images from the first stage of project development.

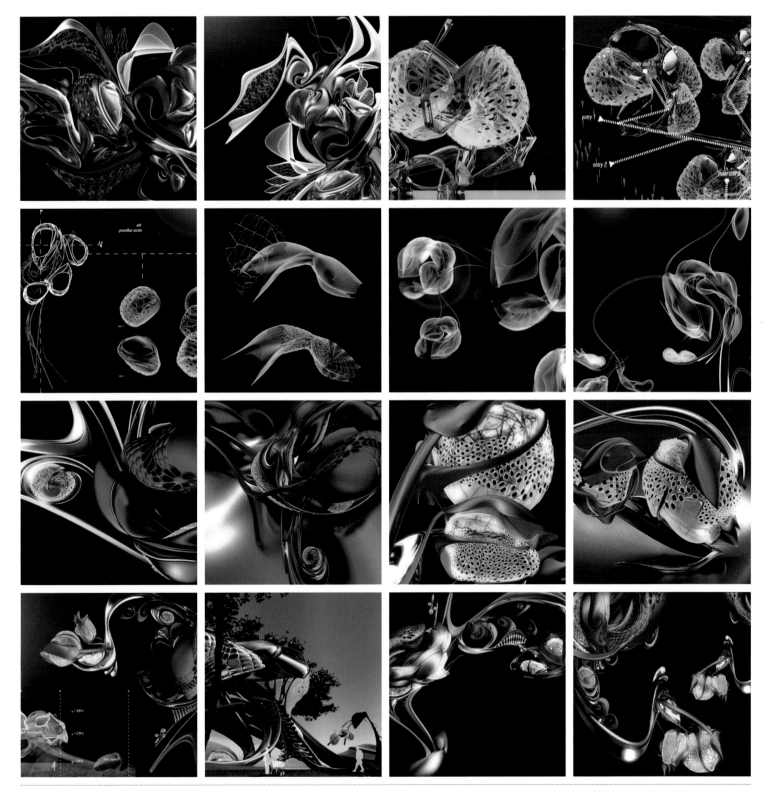

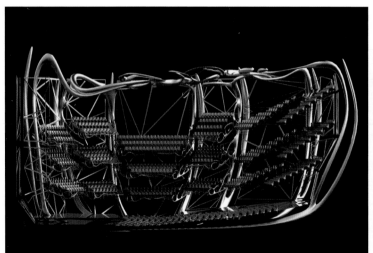

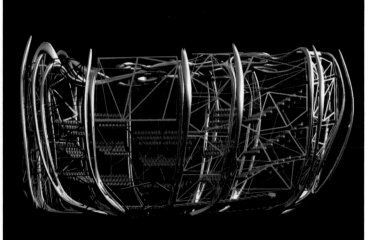

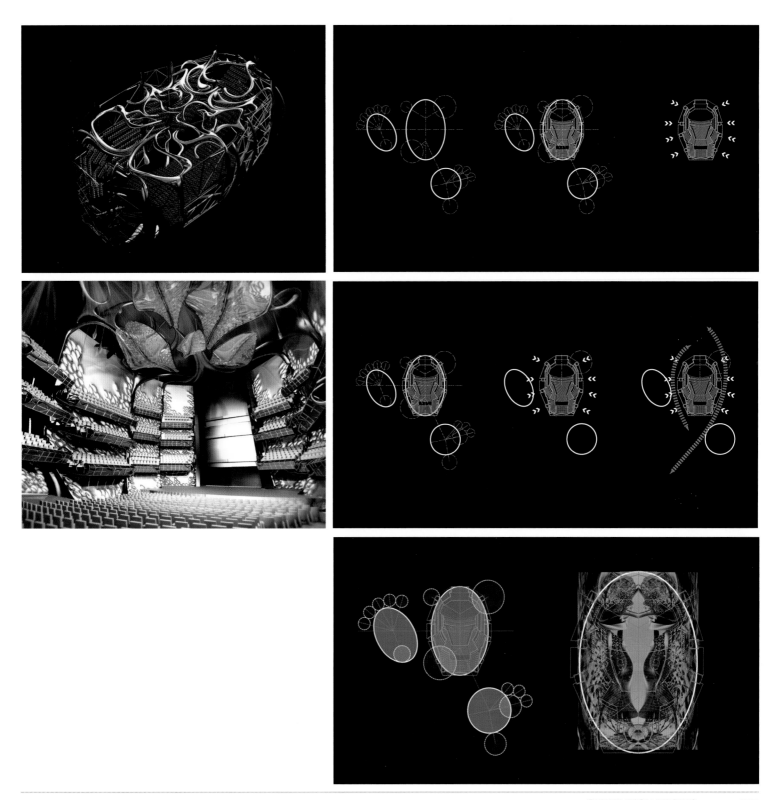

Xing Wang

Haarlem Canal Pavilion

The design proposes a multi-functional pavilion situated at the Nieuwe Gracht in Haarlem, which is approximately 30 meters wide and situated between the city's train station and the city center. The project aims at changing the typical experience of a Dutch canal and providing a landscape architecture above the canal water. Furthermore it generates a large and adjustable interior space for cultural and commercial functions for the neighborhood.

Besides the design for the landscape and its function, the main objective of the project was to explore a solution for a customized parametric building system and to create a non-standard prefabricated structure. Most parts of the building could be fabricated by CNC machine and easily assembled on the site. The design is considered more in terms of customization, BIM and CNC solutions. Then the building could emerge more by itself instead of being drawn.

The concept of this project is to change the straight and flat surroundings of the typical Dutch canal scenery to a more dynamic landscape. The building is a multi-shell geometry which can provide big and continual interior spaces used for shops, conferences and cultural functions. The form finding process of this complex geometry was parametric and customized, which allows both users and owners of a building to join the design process and adjust the geometry with some simple methods and limited variables. The final geometry was selected from the multiple results of this process, according to the functional and structural input.

After the general form finding process, the design needed some further structural and functional development. The roof structure is composed by triangular wooden cells. It consists of two layers: a wooden structure on the outside and on the inside a triangular glass mesh dragged by the steel elements, which are attached to the wooden cells. The production of the wooden shell structure became essential. First, the triangular pattern was applied to the surface and manipulated according to the structure optimization process. Afterwards, the polylines of the triangular pattern were transferred to the 3d triangular wooden cells, which could be man-

ufactured by a CNC machine. The wooden cells can be detailed completely by computer generation, since all construction data was generated by computer. The whole design is adjustable as well since a BIM system could be used. This allows both the designer as the commissioner to take control over the budget.

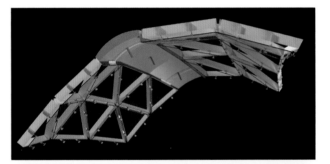

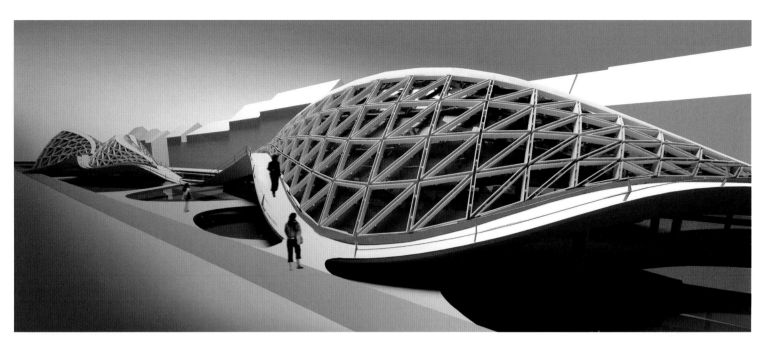

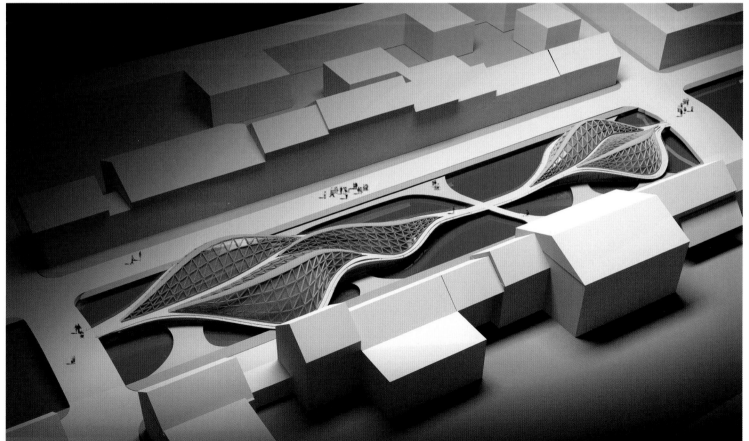

The next step was to develop a direct connection from a 3d digital file to a fabrication and construction file. Parametric software helped to automatically transfer the geometrical data to Rhino CAM. By selecting a group of the wooden cells in the digital model, the computer could directly translate this into milling data needed for a 5 axis milling machine. A CNC machine could cut and mill all the wooden panels with all details. These completely detailed panels could then be assembled fast and precisely in a factory. Small pieces of the shell structure can be pre-assembled before assembling the complete shell structure at the site. Such a construction process could keep building sites as clean as possible. This is particular beneficial to difficult construction circumstances on site, such as the limited working space along Dutch canals.

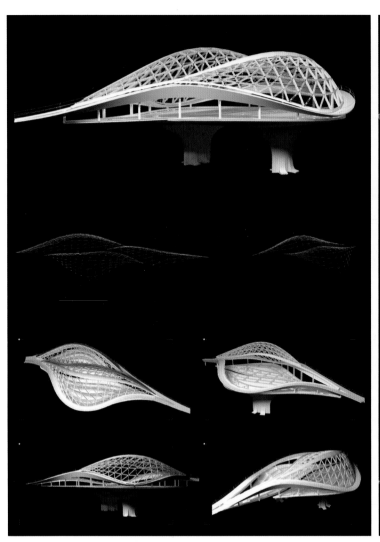
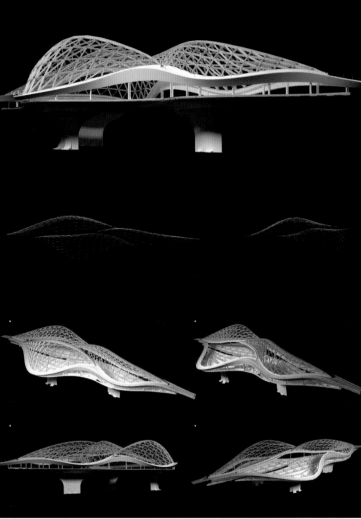

Form-finding process

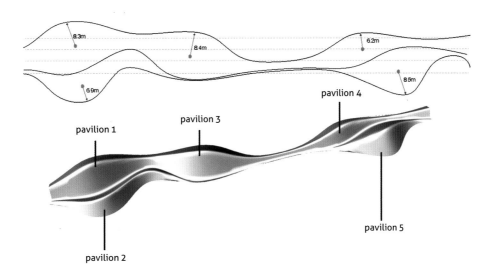

pavilion 1

pavilion 3

pavilion 4

pavilion 5

pavilion 2

Deform curve and surface

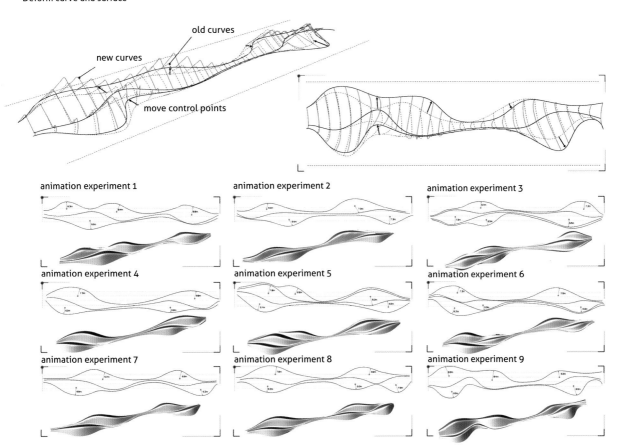

old curves

new curves

move control points

animation experiment 1

animation experiment 2

animation experiment 3

animation experiment 4

animation experiment 5

animation experiment 6

animation experiment 7

animation experiment 8

animation experiment 9

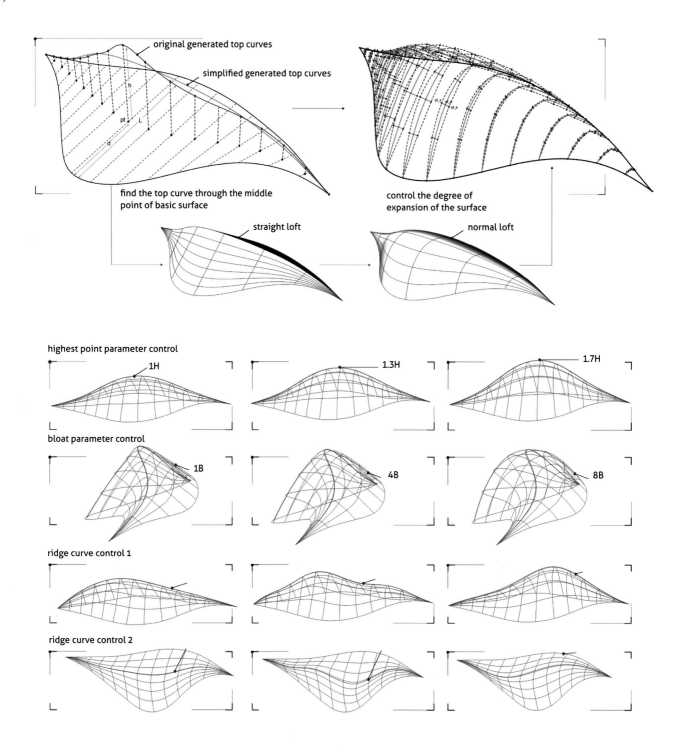

original generated top curves

simplified generated top curves

find the top curve through the middle
point of basic surface

control the degree of
expansion of the surface

straight loft

normal loft

highest point parameter control

1H

1.3H

1.7H

bloat parameter control

1B

4B

8B

ridge curve control 1

ridge curve control 2

Pattern generation

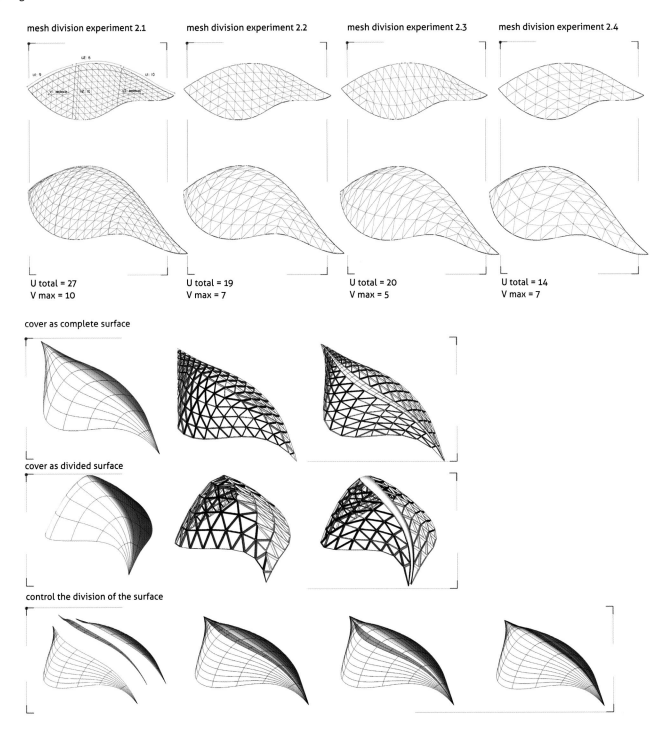

mesh division experiment 2.1   mesh division experiment 2.2   mesh division experiment 2.3   mesh division experiment 2.4

U total = 27
V max = 10

U total = 19
V max = 7

U total = 20
V max = 5

U total = 14
V max = 7

cover as complete surface

cover as divided surface

control the division of the surface

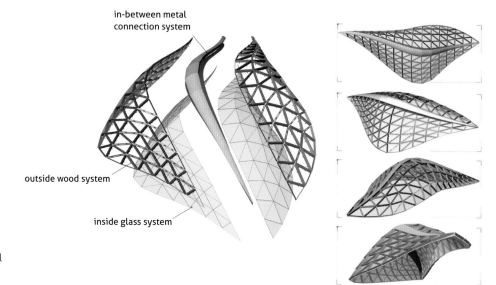

in-between metal
connection system

outside wood system

inside glass system

1. Connector for wood panel
2. Connector for solar panel
3. Connector for moss panel
4. Two-point connector for glass panel
5. Wood panel
6. Laminated glass
7. EPDM sealing
8. Hole for connection between wood panels
9. Hole for connection between wood and metal
10. Milled position for metal connector
11. Metal connector

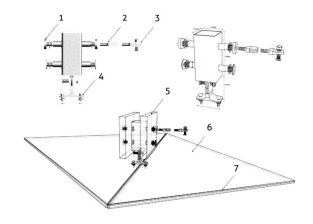

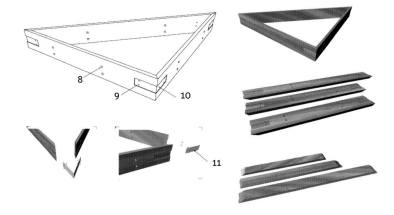

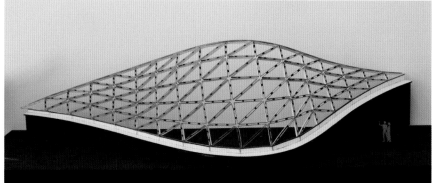

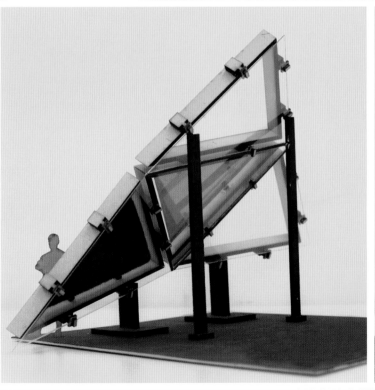

Xing Wang - Matthijs la Roi

Frozen Motion

Spatial developers Bohemen organized the competition A View 4 You, in which participants were required to design a building which, besides having architectural appeal, could profile a brand at a narrow site beside the A4 motorway. The competition was open to students and professional architectural firms.

The designers' aim was to generate a dynamic and non-standard building through a geometric form-finding process and a specific materialization and manufacture logic. *"Walking through this building, visitors could imagine they had become part of an adventure, like 'Jonah in the Whale'. Both the interior and the exterior of the building have a cathedral-like appeal and could bring the Leiden region a completely new kind of world fame,"* the jury report says about Frozen Motion.

The starting concept or diagram comes from the movement of carbon fiber feet. Accompanied by the movement of the feet, the structure itself also generates a gradual deformation. Starting from powerless status to fully weighted status, the structure experiences a different deformation period, when we put each of the frozen motion frames together according to the timeline, it generates a continuous structure system with a gradient transition.

Based on this general concept, the designers organized some physical test to find the relationship between the deformed material and the general geometry. From the gradient control of the bend degree of the ring material, results a continuous surface and the volume inside. Apart from the control of the degree, the designers also controlled the section geometry of the ring frame. Several curves were generated to represent the surface, the space inside, and the divide points from the curves that define the bended ring structure.

Designers: Xing Wang and Matthijs la Roi
Prize: 1st prize of "a view 4 you" competition organized by bohemen
Location: A4 motorway, Leiden, The Netherlands

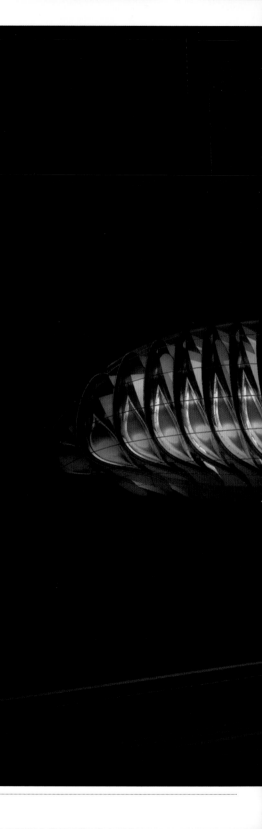

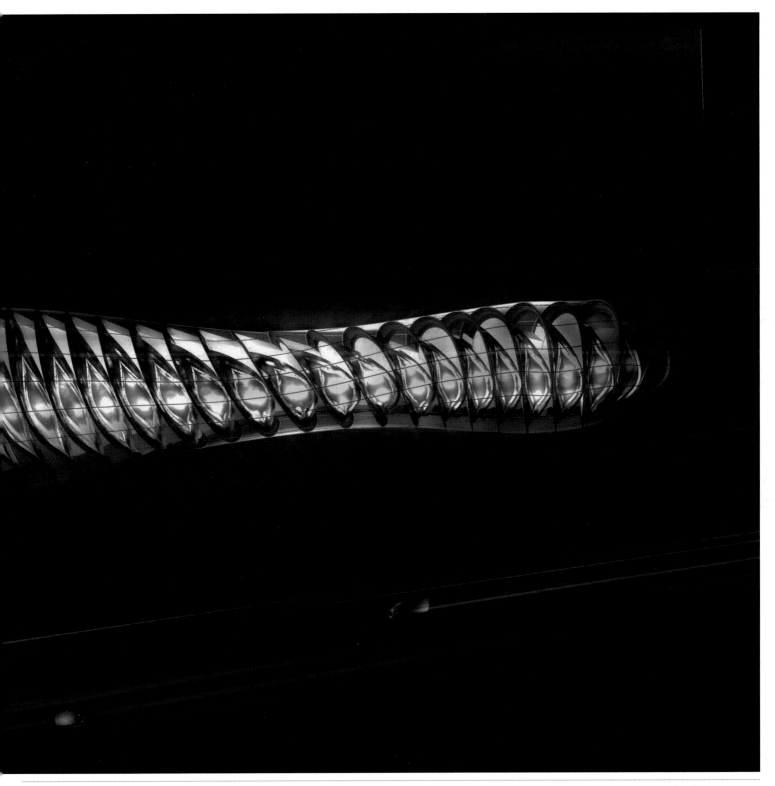

A series of animations was made to record the process, each frame of the regeneration also giving the spatial information such as interior area, material area and number of rooms. According to this information and the relationship between geometry and environment, the designers chose one of the regeneration frames to do the next optimization steps.

Through the physical and digital form finding and test, the optimal geometry emerged by itself. The next step was to go further and control the structure, space and detail generation process precisely and seamlessly. In order to do it, the whole process was divided to several steps. Firstly, the basic curves generated from the last step were simplified and deformed according to the actual program requirements and environmental situation. Then the control points of the bended ring frames emerged from the curves. The next step was to precisely control the wood frame based on the material and real structure. Finally, the 3D computational structure geometry comes out.

The structure contains 3 parts, the wood frame system, the top membrane frame system, and the bottom concrete and steel system. The bottom system supports the steady the wood frame, and the membrane frame system integrates the wood frame together from the top.

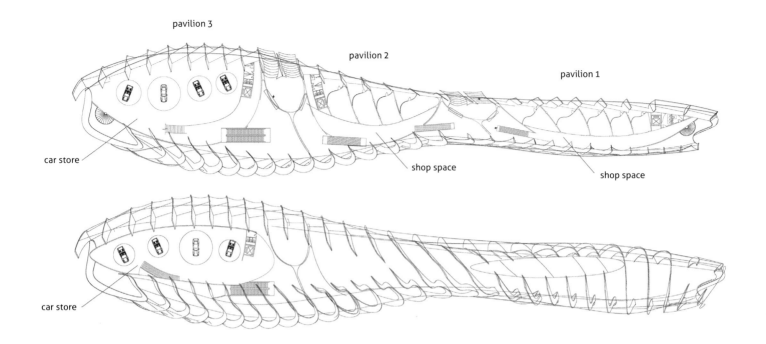

pavilion 3

pavilion 2

pavilion 1

car store

shop space

shop space

car store

deformation of carbon-fiber

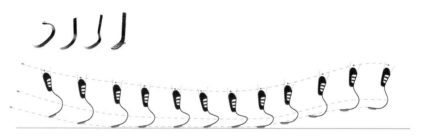

parametric control system

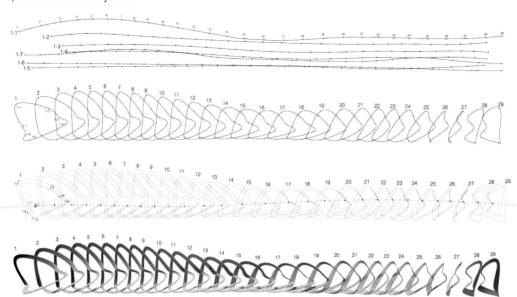

animation simulation and multi-results

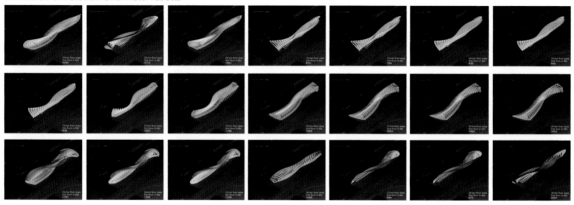

deformation of ring structure

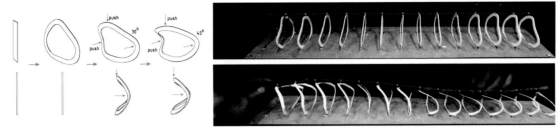

non-standard rings

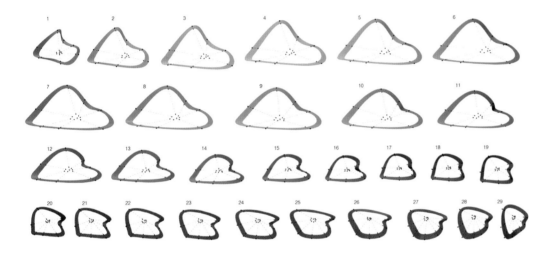

structure system and construction proposal

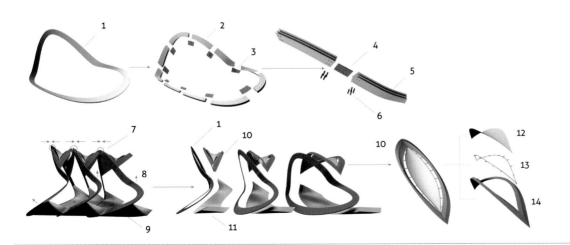

1. Wood frame structure
2. Divided wood panel
3. Connection system
4. Steel connector
5. Three-layered wood panel
6. Rivet
7. Connection of two wood-frame structures
8. Bend force to hold the weight
9. Force to support wood frame structure
10. Light-weight membrane system
11. Concrete and steel structure
12. Membrane material (PTFE)
13. Steel frame structure
14. Fiber glass frame structure

Jaenes Bong – Jonathan Alotto

Puzzling Zenith

Puzzling Zenith concentrates on non-traditional bracing structure. This project proposed the development of a new type of structure with added qualities, that would serve not only as structure but also as ornament. The designers began with triangulated structures that they then made more complicated based on aesthetic rather than structural criteria.

Triangulated structures are rigid and stable and can be adapted to any form. This project is a celebration of the idea of going against the static appearance of a conventional triangulated structure. the design process began with displacing the nodal points of the structure then introducing deliberately random additional points to create a new triangulated mesh. The structural form evolves in response to the contours of the volume being modeled, so that the surface form is like the starting point of a puzzle, the resolution of which is the elaborate, ornate, resultant structure.

Design: Jaenes Bong – Jonathan Alotto
Location: Nouméa, New Caledonia

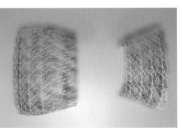

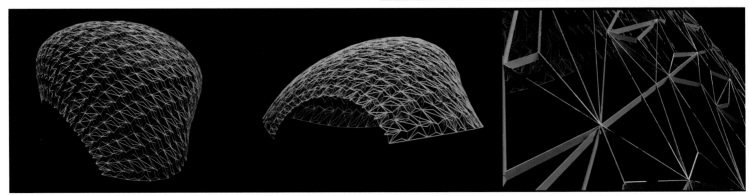

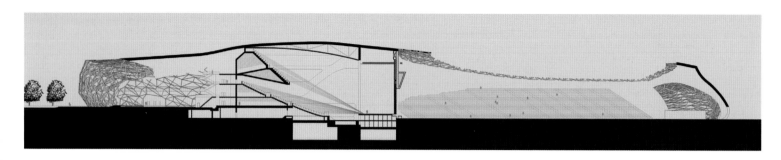

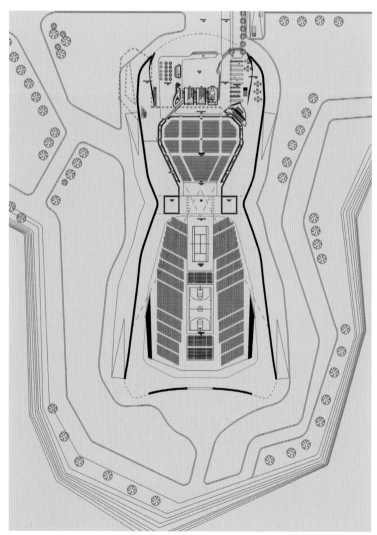

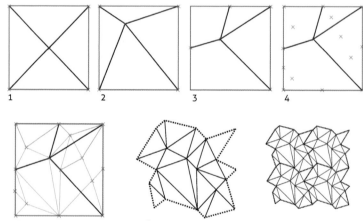

1. Traditional counter-bracing
2. Distortion of the crossing point
3. Displacement of the four crossing points
4. Positioning deliberate random points
5. Connecting points to create triangulated mesh system within each zone
6. Defining the puzzle profile contour
7. Puzzling the mesh group onto freeform application

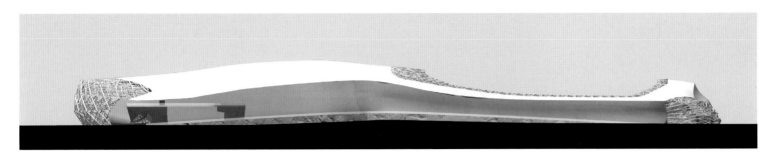

moh architects

Evolutionary Computation

Form follows function. This famous and disputed demand, associated mainly with architectural modernism in the 20th century, seems to be most valid when looking at biological systems. In these systems the form and structure of a biological entity equips the organism best for survival. In order to succeed, biological structures are highly complex systems with the aim of reaching an optimized solution for any given requirement. Every organism and life form emerges through the process of evolutionary self-organization.

While the principles of morphogenesis tend to become an increasingly attractive paradigm in the field of architectural design and the aesthetic appeal of natural form has always been important to architects and designers, the inherent principles of these systems have gained significance ever since evolutionary and genetic computation have become utilized for design and optimization purposes.

The project investigates the potential offered by evolutionary and genetic computation towards a more holistic approach in architectural and structural design. It takes advantage of evolutionary form finding strategies through the use of material self organization under load and gravity. Instead of relying on post-optimizing the structure in the final stage of the process, the project embraces these methods as great opportunities and deliberately deploys them as the very tools of the design.

Evolutionary and genetic computation strategies are used for finding an optimized form (based on given demands) and finally leading to a differentiated and complex architectural result.

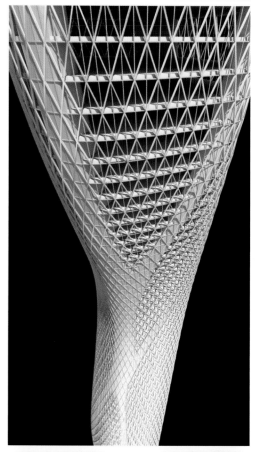

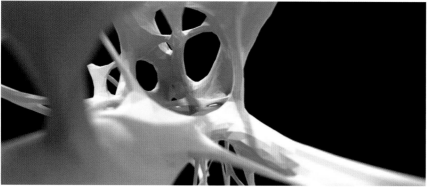

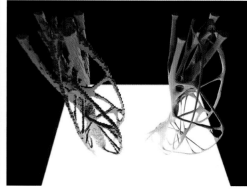

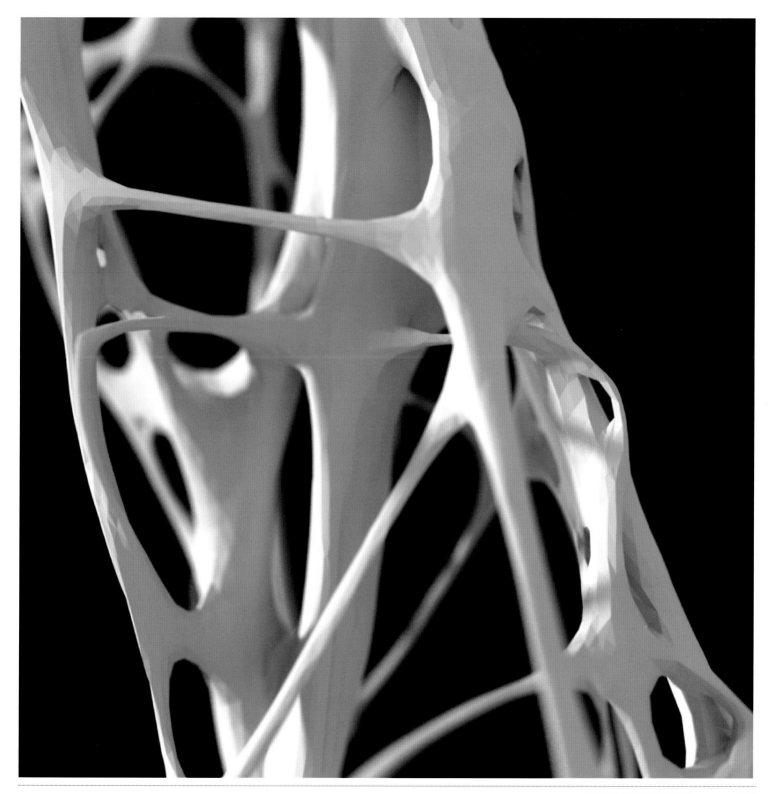

Evolutionary optimization

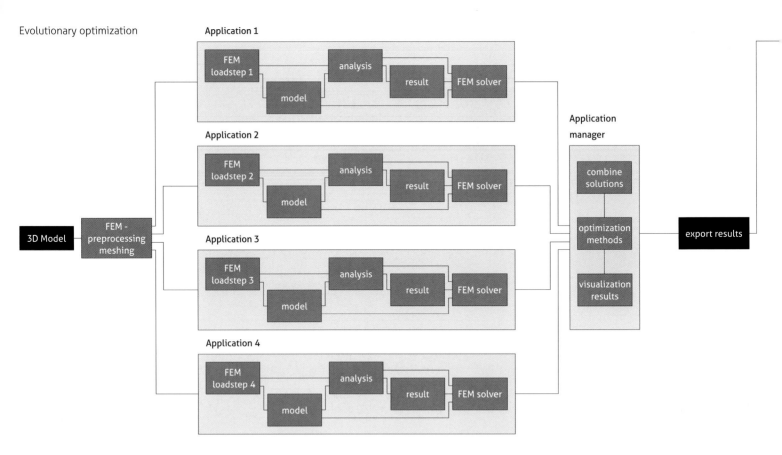

Application 1
FEM loadstep 1 — analysis — result — FEM solver — model

Application 2
FEM loadstep 2 — analysis — result — FEM solver — model

Application 3
FEM loadstep 3 — analysis — result — FEM solver — model

Application 4
FEM loadstep 4 — analysis — result — FEM solver — model

3D Model — FEM - preprocessing meshing

Application manager
combine solutions
optimization methods
visualization results

export results

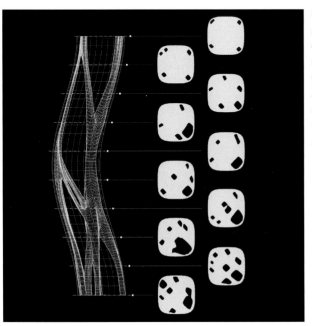

Design space: Initial space for the structural optimization and the resulting core
Core: The core acts as a structural and vertical organization system
Envelope: The envelope is a self-supporting structure

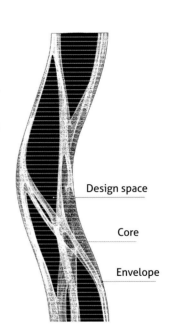

Design space

Core

Envelope

1. Initial structure
2. Cellular automata grid
3. Cellular automata rule
4. Resulting structure
5. Cellular automata cells
6. Resulting geometry

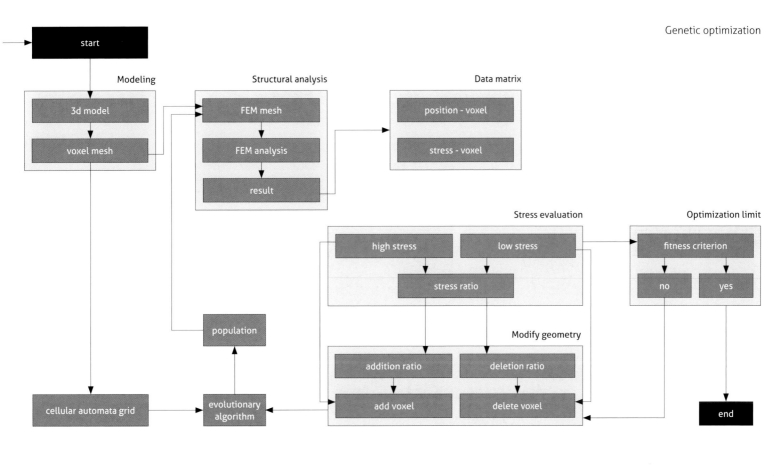

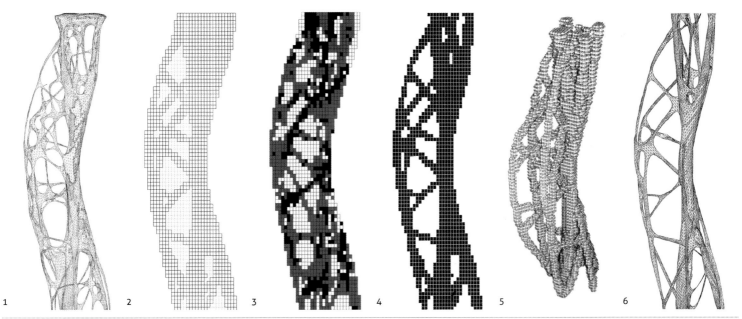

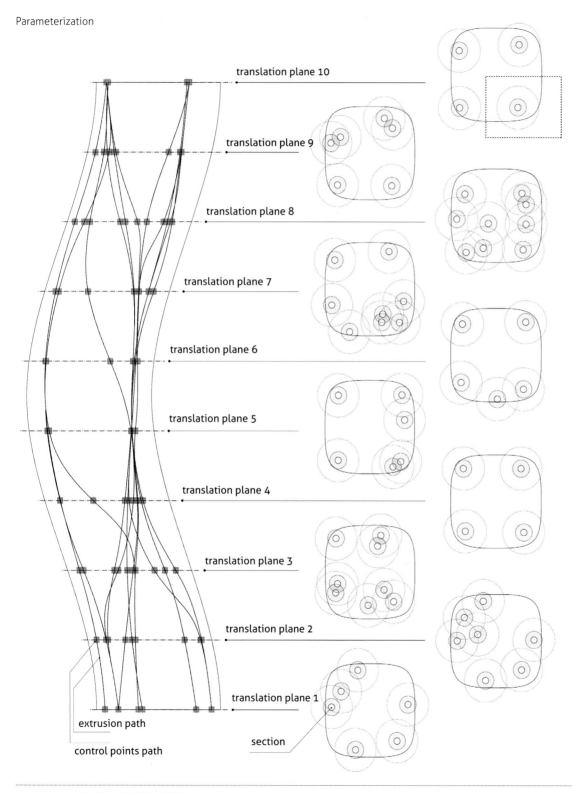

translation plane 10

translation plane 9

translation plane 8

translation plane 7

translation plane 6

translation plane 5

translation plane 4

translation plane 3

translation plane 2

translation plane 1

extrusion path

control points path

section

1. Pointcloud
2. Point selection
3. Point extraction
4. Reorganized points
5. Approximation curves
6. Extrusion
7. Basic geometry
8. Geometry with design variables
9. Points with direction vector
10. Translation vector
11. Amount of translation
12. Main translation points

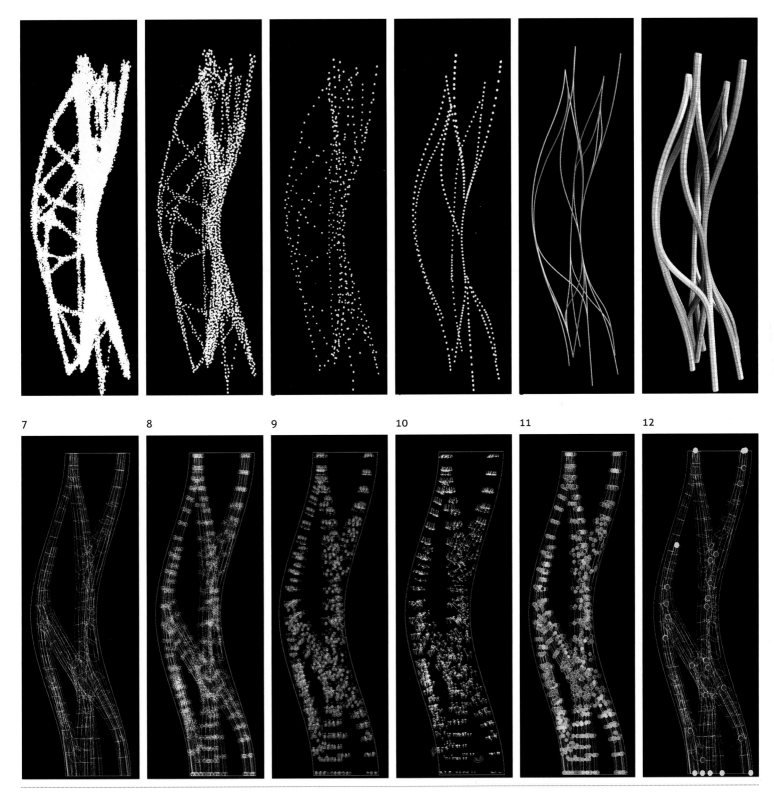

7 8 9 10 11 12

SDA

Pushkinsky Cinema

The design of the Pushkinsky Cinema façade renovation places the face of the landmark venue behind a sculptural veil which acts as a dramatic backdrop to Pushkin Square and an iconic face to the cinema. Inspired by the screened views, geometric intricacy and flowing surfaces of a "Russian Veil", the design contrasts the imposing presence of the Brutalist architectural icon by simultaneously enclosing and revealing its contents behind a delicate yet robust open air lattice materialized as thermo-formed sheets of DuPont Corian. The solid mass of the building is clad in a series of Corian panels which gently morph the relentless diagrid pattern of the existing façade into a flowing and varied matrix of warped hexagon modules.

The composite effect of the varied orientations of the hexagonal screen components creates a rich and dramatic moiré effect which dissolves from opaque to transparent and back again as one moves around, through and within the building. With each step the building appears to change through the interplay of light, shadow, and visual connectivity as the thin 13mm thick Corian sheets nearly disappear upon perpendicular viewing while those at oblique angles to the viewer are revealed through their 500mm depth. This dynamic effect encourages visual interaction and connectivity between the cinema and Pushkin Square by simultaneously revealing and concealing the contents of the cinema through a multiplicity of varying and directed views into and out of the lobby.

In addition to its stunning visual performance, the screen wall also acts as a brise-soleil providing solar shading to protect the clear glazed lobby, while providing for ample opportunities for indirect day lighting. As the geometry evolves from diagrid to hex, subtle shifts in rotation, scale, and connectivity occur which further articulate the pattern to include varying densities and orientations of the apertures in response to annual solar incidence on the façade surface. Greater density is achieved where required, and greater transparency where it is not necessary. This gradient of articulation results in a spectacular dappled shading effect mirroring the visual moiré.

Design: SDA | Synthesis Design + Architecture
Location: Moscow, Russia
Date: 2011

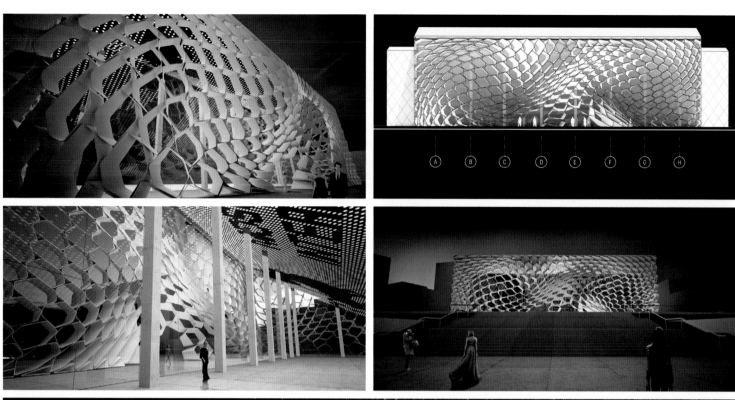

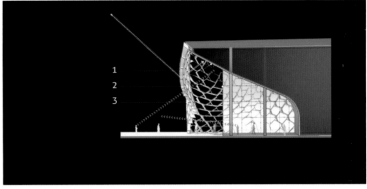

View vectors
1. Views out
2. Views in/out
3. Views in

Screen wall section
1. LED multimedia ceiling display
2. Sentryglass frameless glazing system
3. Thermo-formed Corian screen wall

A. Hanging slot detail
1. Stainless steel plate with hanging slots
2. Stainless steel plate with welded studs
3. Corian squirrel fixings

B. Modular assembly concept
4. Hexagonal Corian modules
5. Fixing plates
6. Triangular Corian base plates with anchors

C. Thermoforming concept
7. Fixed radius cylindrical formers
8. 13 mm thermoformed glacier white Corian
9. CNC milled Corian sheet (unrolled)

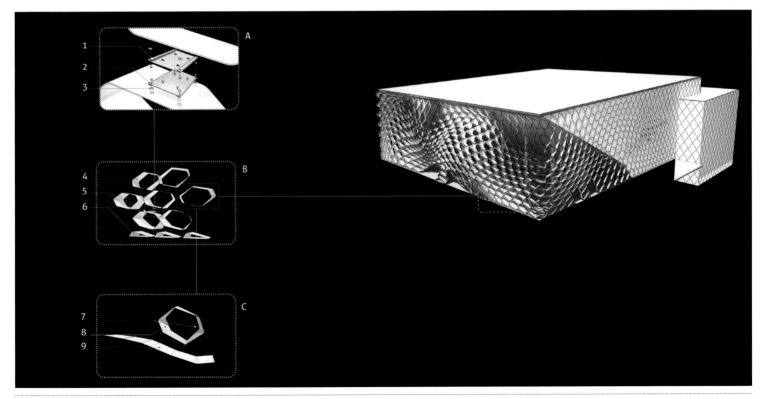

su11 architecture+design

Dervish Tower

Dervish Tower is a prototype for a high-riser with a distinctly animated building envelope. Inspired by the surface effects generated through rotational movement, this tower features an ambiguous overall shape as well as a façade with parametrically controlled panelization.

On the macro-scale the tower's whirling shape breaks with the straight building edges usually associated with high-risers. Instead the building surface produces a continuously changing outline through which qualities of motion and plasticity are expressed.

On the micro-scale the skin of the project is based on a large number of individual panels. These panels consist of glass, metal, and solar cells. Each of them has a different angular shape and is controlled by a set of rotation-based rules, which provide closure, shading, and aperture.

The parametric façade paneling setup allows for a reciprocal relationship between the overall curvature of the envelope surface and the offset angles of the individual panels. Stronger undulations in the surface translate into greater angularity, which in turn results in larger apertures. The design of the façade is thus orchestrated through the feedback of surface movement into gradual component proliferation.

The scale-like effects further accentuate the tower's shifting atmospheres. Responding to different times of the day, the façade changes its appearance from transparent to opaque and from a metallic-monochromatic shade to a colorful and reflective one.

Partners in charge: Ferda Kolatan & Erich Schoenenberger
Design team: Matt Lake, Andy Lucia, Kyu Chun

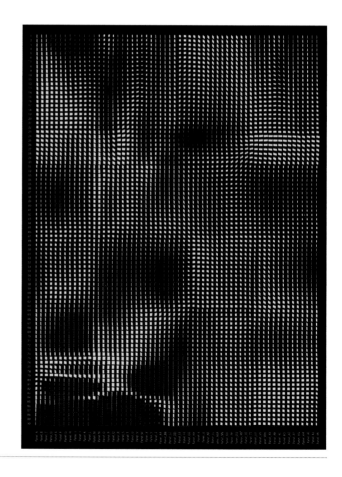

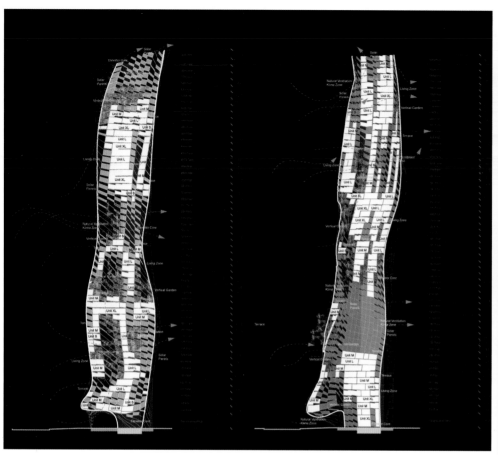

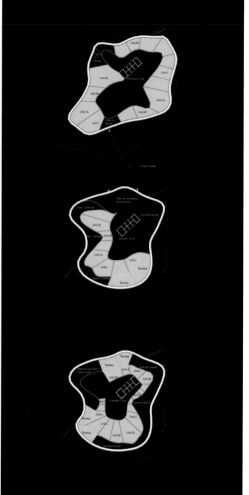

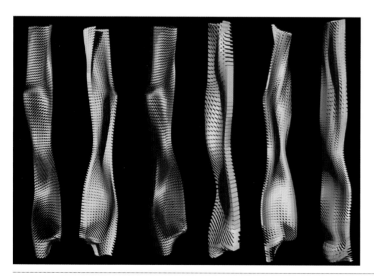

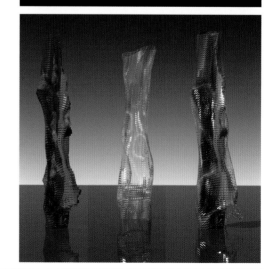

su11 architecture+design

Pluripotent Design Strategies / PS_Canopy

Pluripotent: Not fixed as to developmental potentialities.

Dictionary.com

The evolution of form occurs through changes in development.

Sean B. Carroll

Pluripotent Structures describe a series of experimental investigations we have been conducting into more adaptive and variable design systems, which take advantage of multi-scalar and parametric techniques to generate formal organizations that challenge conventional architectural categorizations such as structure, volume and surface. Instead, these investigations focus on regionally customizable models, which maintain an overall design coherence while also displaying local specificity. Every one of these models has multiple potentialities and can be further refined through continuous feed-back loops. This approach is equally driven by the testing of unprecedented design methodologies as it is by the search for novel and unexpected expressions in architecture. As many of the advanced computational techniques mature, more distinct and deliberate applications are necessary to examine the larger ramifications and effects of these prototypes.

PS_Canopy is one of these prototypes that have taken this investigation into a specific scale, program, and materiality. Taking cues from Biologist Sean B. Carroll's description of "Body Part" development in nature, PS_Canopy seeks to provide continual variations through the implementation of parametric dependencies. Carroll argues that any novelty of body-parts is based not on innovation but "rather a matter of modifying existing structures and of teaching old genes how to learn new tricks". These tricks, he reasons are achieved by switching on and off so-called toolkit genes at different times and places through the course of cell development. If difference is created through a large number of combinatorial and incremental changes within a relatively manageable set of building blocks, a resourceful yet limitless design methodology can be formulated.

Partners in charge: Ferda Kolatan & Erich Schoenenberger
Design team: Richard Baxley, Hart Marlow

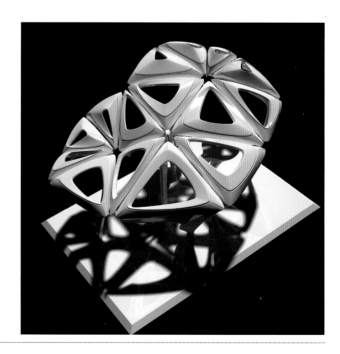

PS_Canopy operates on two distinct and growth based principles. The first one determines overall size, distribution, and density of the individual cellular components. The second one focuses on the internal transformation of these components into different performative parts. The canopy consists of three main parts, which in a morphological reference to flowers are called stem, petal, and leaf. The architectural definition of these translates into structure/post, shade, and seating/counter. The original setup provides for a basic organization with latent possibilities to generate any number of stems, petals, and leafs in multiple scales with formal and functional variations. The model is open-ended as it can be adjusted and refined without its core constituents being altered.

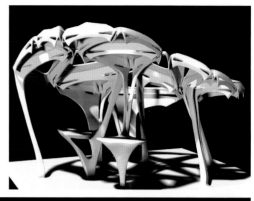

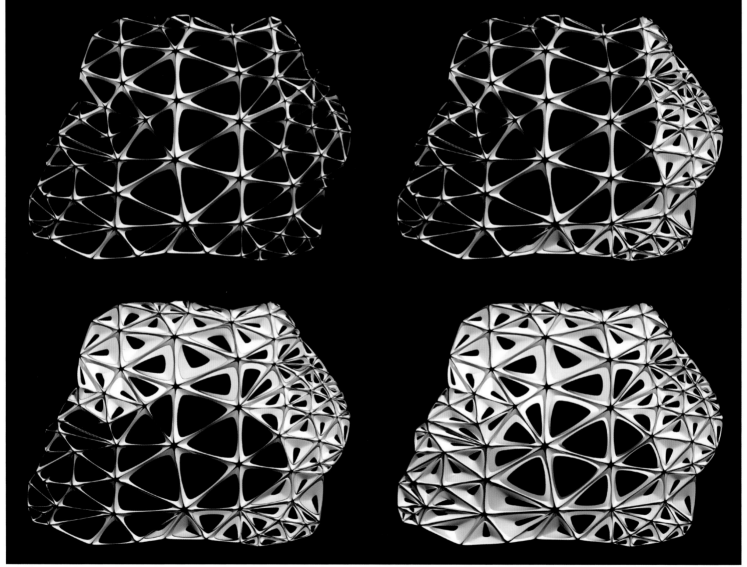

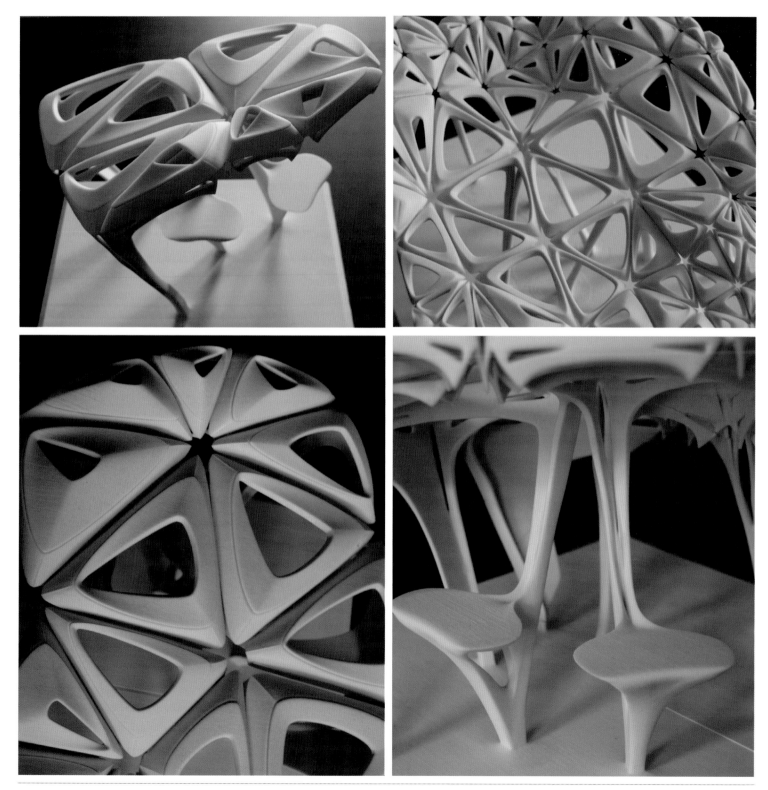

Studio BÄNG

Bridging the Gap

The design of this bridge developed from Studio BÄNG's investigation into digital design manufacturing methods and the idea of creating a bridge that looks complex but is easy to construct. The design process began by defining as parametric points positions that were key to the bridge's structural, constructional and functional efficiency. Parameterizing these twelve points located at the ends and in the center of the bridge enabled the designers to control the resulting structure. The framework was then distorted in relation to sun angles. An operation known as "lofting" was subsequently performed on the resulting curves to achieve highly rigid and complex-looking shapes that could be fabricated from thin steel sheets laser cut and seamed.

The parametric process has resulted in a bridge design that is entirely independent of site conditions. Designed to be manufactured in parts, it is a structure that is well suited to use in mountain areas. The triangular modules could be prefabricated and transported to the site by helicopter for assembly, which would require only two workers.

The designers used the Rhino Nest plug-in for Grasshopper to generate the cutting pattern for the steel sheets, complete with holes for the connection bolts. An angle-calculating component was also inserted into the definition of the pieces so that the angles for the folds in the pieces would be automatically fed into to the electronic press brake.

After receiving the laser cut and pressed pieces from the factory, they would be bolted together to form three modules. In the case of the model this took one hour. The modules would then be transported to the site. Two workers would be able to install the bridge and bolt the modules together in less than 2 days. The whole assembly process of the 1:5 scale model took five hours. After installation, a steel grating would be inserted to serve as the floor surface.

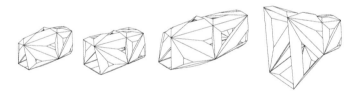

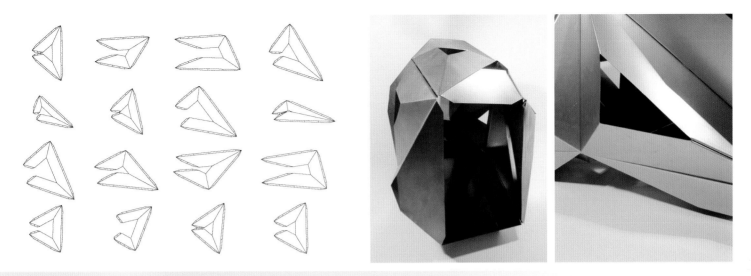

Tommaso Casucci

Biodigital Processes In Architecture

The project for the new library of the school of Architecture in Florence is a study case about biodigital processes in Architectural design. The project explores the qualities of surfaces modulation driven by intensive datascapes describing environmental conditions on a building site.

At the same time, the project aims to define an intelligent material distribution through space as a balanced combination of physical matter, geometry and energy of the system. This kind of material intelligence is very frequent in Biology:

"Biology makes use of remarkably few materials, (...) and they have much lower densities than most engineering materials. They are successful not so much because of what they are but because of the way they are put together." [1].

The building site is located at the limit of the old city of Florence and it is part of a renovation plan of a large area used until recent times as convent and later prison.

Pre-existing spaces of the prison are converted into an archive, the new extension includes study areas, meeting rooms, an auditorium and exhibition spaces.

1. George Jeronimidis , Biodynamics, Architectural Design Magazine, Vol. 74, Wiley, 2004

Design: Tommaso Casucci
Supervisor: Alessio Erioli, Ulisse Tramonti
Location: Florence, Italy

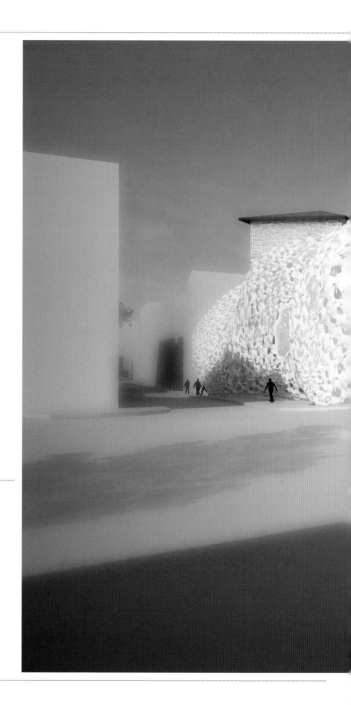

Ground floor plan (1-1')

Second floor plan (3-3')

Section C-C'

Section A-A'

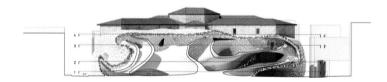

Section D-D'

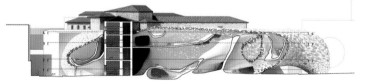

Section B-B'

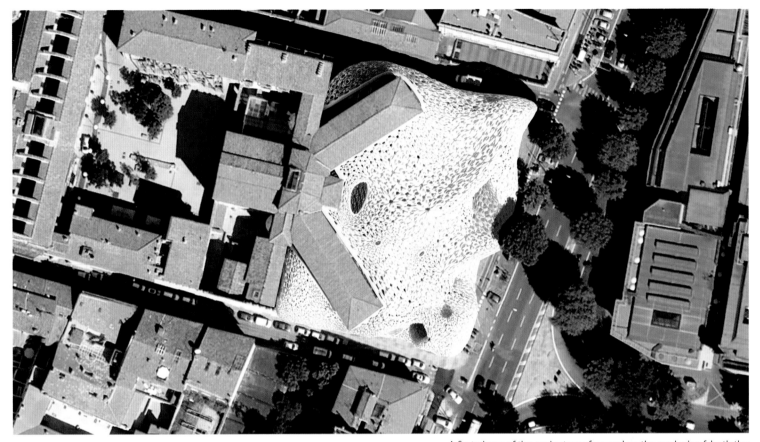

A first phase of the project was focused on the analysis of both the current state and future projections of the specific environmental conditions on the building site. In this phase a large quantity of relevant data was collected and structured to set up a 3d vector field describing the environmental datascape. In particular road system, traffic conditions, users´ access expectations and digital 3d environment reconstruction.

Elevation - Via Ghibellina

Elevation - Viale della Giovine Italia

Elevation - Via dell' Angolo

During the second phase the defined globular shape of the library was based on the extraction of isosurfaces describing equipotential conditions inside the 3D vector field. Among various generated solutions the one that shows the most efficient compromise between surface planarity and wider range of spatial differentiation was then selected.

On a finer scale, surfaces porosity was also defined in order to regulate climatic conditions and light perception in the interior spaces of the library. This system is based on the parametrically controlled proliferation of a particular kind of triply periodic minimal surface, the Schoen's Manta Surface. Triply periodic minimal surfaces are a particular family of minimal surfaces whose structure is based on a three dimensional crystalline organization in space.

Schoen's Manta Surface structure, in particular, is based on the three dimensional repetition of a simple cubical cell. Proliferation of this module on different types of quad-based meshes give rise to interesting emerging effect on the whole proliferation.

Phenotypical variation of the basic cell was finally defined according to direct solar radiation values derived from solar analysis. The variation of components through the surface modulates solar gain in the interior spaces of the library fostering the passage of direct solar rays in low values areas and conversely fostering the passage of scattered light in high values areas.

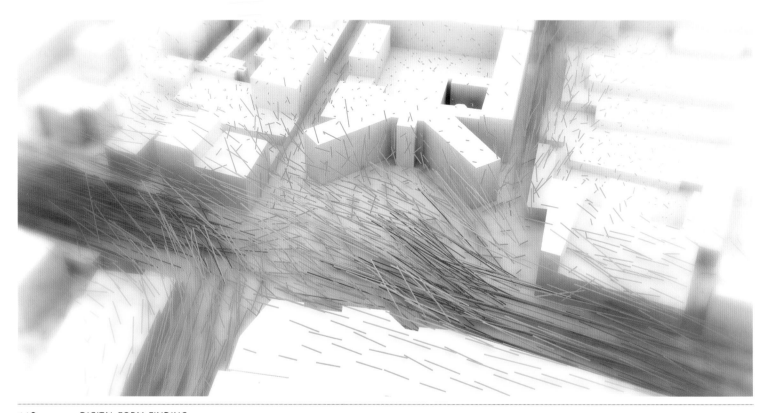

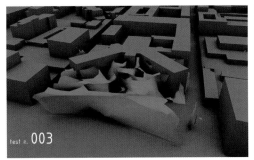

test n. 003

field selection value: 0.1
mesh selection value: 0.25
polygons: 1604

test n. 005

field selection value: 0.1
mesh selection value: 0.45
polygons: 1614

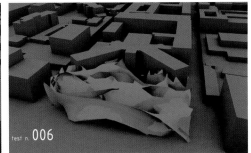

test n. 006

field selection value: 0.2
mesh selection value: 0.05
polygons: 1491

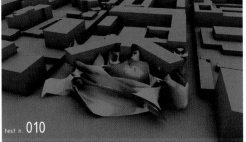

test n. 010

field selection value: 0.2
mesh selection value: 0.45
polygons: 1630

test n. 011

field selection value: 0.3
mesh selection value: 0.05
polygons: 1640

test n. 014

field selection value: 0.3
mesh selection value: 0.35
polygons: 1520

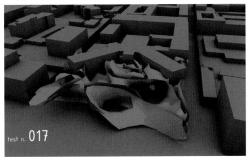

test n. 017

field selection value: 0.4
mesh selection value: 0.15
polygons: 1628

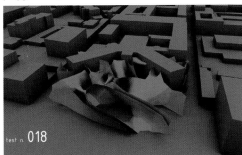

test n. 018

field selection value: 0.4
mesh selection value: 0.25
polygons: 1484

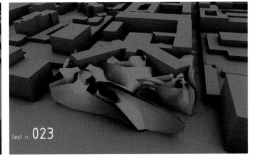

test n. 023

field selection value: 0.5
mesh selection value: 0.25
polygons: 1529

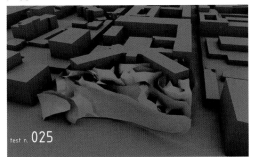

test n. 025

field selection value: 0.5
mesh selection value: 0.45
polygons: 1534

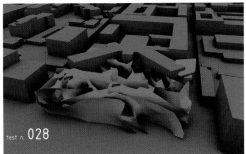

test n. 028

field selection value: 0.6
mesh selection value: 0.25
polygons: 1704

test n. 029

field selection value: 0.6
mesh selection value: 0.35
polygons: 1826

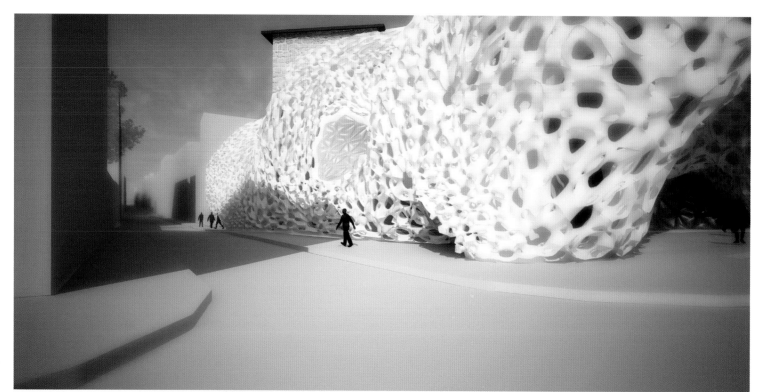

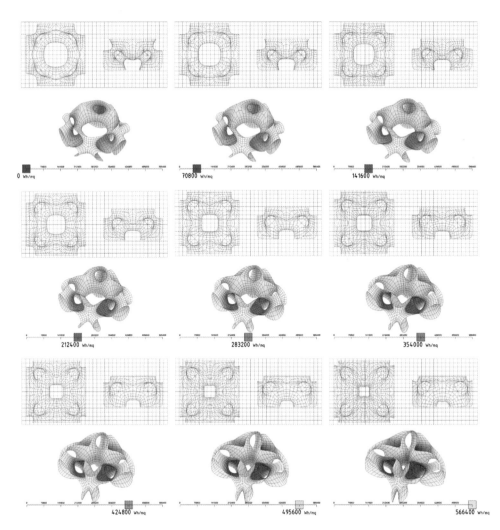

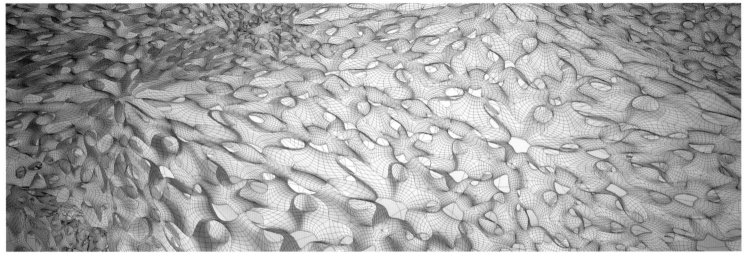

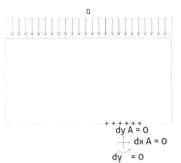

$dy\, A = 0$

$dx\, A = 0$

$dy\; = 0$

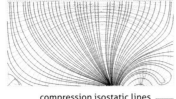

compression isostatic lines ——
tension isostatic lines ——

optimized material density

steps: 12
target density: 0.010
penalization: 3.000
filtering: 1

derived mesh

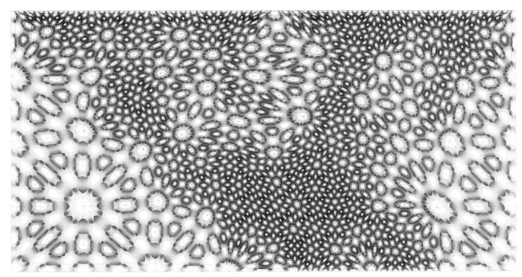

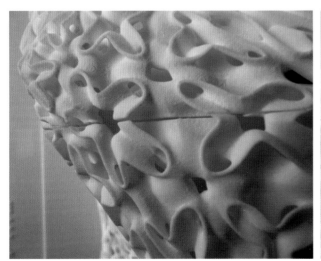

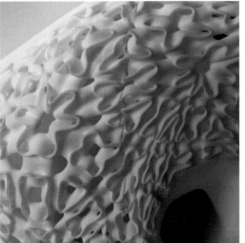

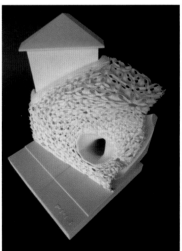

Sustainable Technologies

The common discourse on sustainability sees technology as problematic. Many designers that seek sustainability turn to traditional designs and construction methods where they find answers to problems created by contemporary methods of designing and constructing. But there is another view of sustainability, one that embraces technology and tries to find solutions through its clever application. The embrace of technology gives the opportunity to design on a greater scale and to envision solutions that require not only technological advancement but social change in order to be implemented. Such proposals may work as a critique of the commonly accepted notion of sustainability showing that the issue is more than technical; there are social, economic and political factors that need to be addressed for sustainability to be achieved.

One common ancestor of many digital architecture trends is the megastructure architecture of the 60s. Many ideas of digital architecture like the understanding of a building as a system more that an object, the open ended character of the design process, the fusion of architecture and engineering and the understanding of the final object of the design as something malleable and changeable derive from the 60s. But it is in these projects that address the issue of sustainability that the debt to the past becomes clear while at the same time it becomes obvious how many things have moved forward. Most of the architecture of the 60s was designed under a spell of abundance and innocence. Energy, water and other natural resources were considered as given and their management was seldom thought of. Today, architects are working under a very different spell; innocence about environmental issues is no longer possible and even designs that may remind us of the most fanciful Archigram experiments are actually carrying a far heavier conceptual luggage and enter the discussion about sustainability far more seriously than they may appear to at first sight.

The project **Floating Permaculture** by **Arphenotype** blurs the boundaries between floating permacultures and inhabitable megastructures, blending the ideas and visions of the Metabolists with a process of energy and food production that is based on cybernetics, a science developed by Norbert Wiener in roughly the same period as Metabolism.

Cybernetics as described by Wiener deals with 'control and communication in animal and machine', and this opens the way for effectively combining ecology and technology in floating permaculture, creating dynamic balances and eliminating negative feedback loops. Due to the human involvement in the system, it is what von Foerster calls second order cybernetics. The first order of cybernetics deals with outside observation of the system, while in the second order the observer of the system is part of the system he or she observes. Floating permaculture focuses on second-order cybernetics, because man is always and inevitably a part of the system.

Bringing together a fusion of technological, economical and cultural entities, and combining a public free space into an interlocked modular construct, which includes an internal courtyard as public landscape, the newly developed **(RE)Configured-Assemblage** by **Wendy W Fok** of **WE-DESIGNS.ORG** and **Judith Mussel** of **XP&** becomes an open playground of hidden gems, which offers the community countless integrated opportunities to develop and harmonise the City of Long Beach.

Lorene Faure and **Kenny Kinugasa-Tsui** of **Horhizon** developed **Archifoliage Veils** starting from the following thoughts: "*The rapid development of innovative technological approaches in the realm of biology, biomechanics, biotechnology, aerodynamics, and hydrodynamics are becoming of immense significance to architecture, demanding our attention due to their inevitable cultural, aesthetic and technical implications. This results in the 'biologicalization' phenomenon in architecture. The line between natural and the artificial is progressively blurred.*"

Kadri Kerge – Jenny Chow – Wendy W Fok | WE-DESIGNS.ORG

UP – Tower Transformation

UP is a multilayered investigative study of an urban tower condition, operated under the logics of the hexagon, through a process of developmental delineation studies formed and translated from two-dimensional studies that entered into a three-dimensional rationale, and then developed into an accentuated folded landscape. The folding landscapes of the public space and residential tower offer a bold and playful character of extending the ground plan into a multi-storey tower, and integrated within an urban context—as an urban park within the sky. This folding landscape is achieved by a systematically articulated folding system that is structurally economical, thereby increasing useable floor area, overcoming traditional tectonic and structural hierarchies.

The folding landscape of the public space offers a lively place for social activity and interaction, while bringing nature closer to the user and within each level of space. The dips and dives of the multi-level open public space allows for various public and community programs, while the geometries continually develop spaces of openness and privacy that humanize the scale of the project. The manner in which the public space and tower folds and intertwines into and out of itself and through the site poetically mimics the rolling landscape of the seaside, while integrating natural greenery into the urban spectrum.

In essence, the multifaceted façade of the tower offers beautiful views for the residences, while it discreetly processes, collects, and recycles natural rain through the roof and piping system that is integrated within the design of the folding slabs as an effective social generator.

Studio: WE-DESIGNS.ORG
Design team: Kadri Kerge, Wendy W Fok
Project team: Jenny Chow, Sue Biolsi
Assistants: Viktorie Senesova, Vasilis Raptis (intern)
Client: Surrey Town Planning, Canada
Location: Semiahmoo, Surrey BC, Canada

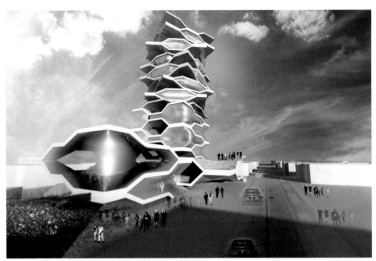

Within the folding system is an integrated piping system that processes, collects, and recycles the rainwater and grey water within the building, and re-uses the water for heating and non-potent water use. This discreet sustainable and self-generating system allows the building to maintain itself without a secondary water supplier, thus can effectively maintain social awareness without being outwardly 'green'.

The use of Bio-glass as a material and the form of the window curvature is designed in a dualistic approach to maximum the thermal absorbance of sun light and balances the performance between reflectivity and materiality. In effect neutralizes the heat in the summer and maximizes the warmth for the winters.

Typologies: Residential tower

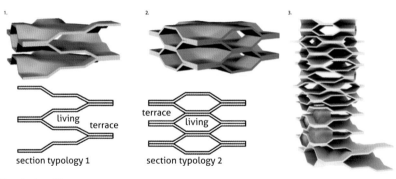

section typology 1   section typology 2

Typologies: Plaza

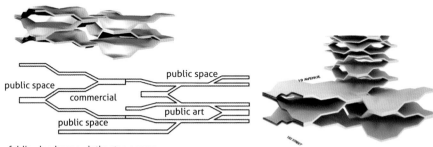

folding landscape - intimate vs open

Folding concept diagrams

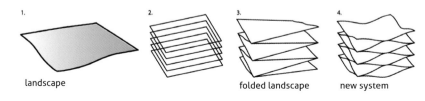

landscape   folded landscape   new system

Intertwined / folded landscape parks

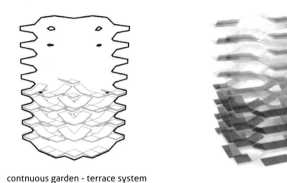

contnuous garden - terrace system

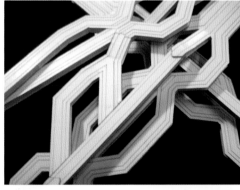

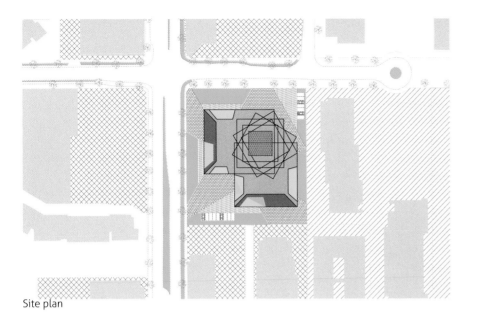

Site plan

Typical residential floor plan

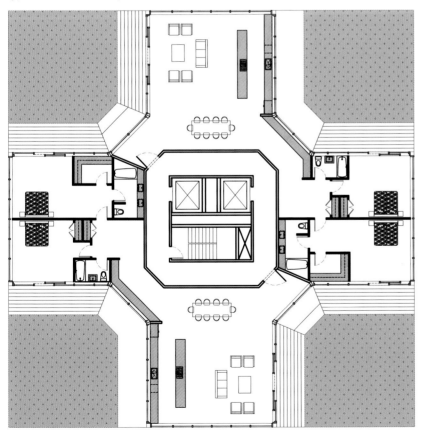

The window and structural frame of the building is intended to be constructed with Bio-Luminum frames and Bio-Glass window Panels. The Bio-Luminum tiles are made from salvaged parts from retired airplanes and are an excellent long-lasting and high-strength material. Bio-Glass is engineered from recycled glass with no additives or colorants. Both materials will contribute towards LEED certification.

While the overall structural construction of the building is constructed by fibrous concrete, the networks or matrices of fibers and fibrils intertwine and cling together with the power of the hydrogen bond mixture of 60% Portland Cement 40% recycled synthetic-fiber (nylon, glass, steel or polypropylene) reinforcement. The technical development of synthetic-fiber reinforcement avoids the increased labor costs and difficulty in placement that are associated with welded-wire fabric (WWF).

Synthetic-fiber reinforcement prevents cracks in concrete, which controls crack width -- cracks actually need to occur before the WWF goes to work. Small-diameter recycled synthetic fibers (nylon, glass, steel or polypropylene) added to concrete reduces shrinkage cracking by more than 80% according to independent lab tests. Reducing cracks improves concrete impermeability, increases its toughness and long-term weatherability, and can reduce callbacks in concrete slab floors, decks, driveways, and walks. According to fiber manufacturers, the placement, curing, or finish characteristics of the concrete are not affected by the addition of fibrous reinforcement.

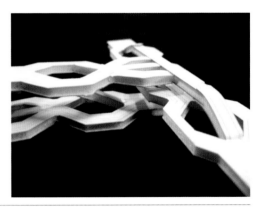

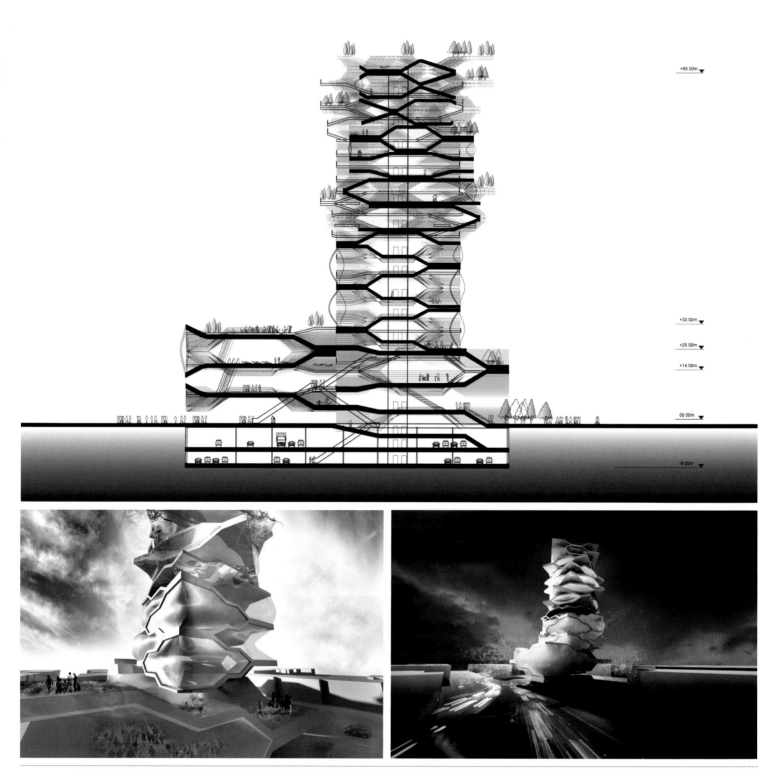

1. Interior finish
2. Thermal insulation
3. Bio-luminium window frame
4. Fibrous concrete slab
5. Bio-glass window panels

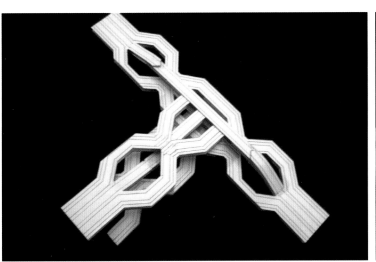
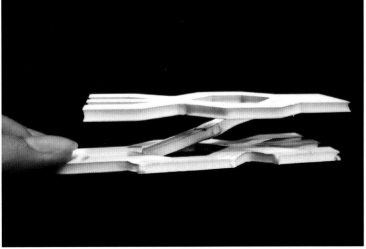

Wendy W Fok | WE-DESIGNS.ORG – Judith Mussel | XP& Architecture

(RE)Configured-Assemblage

(RE)Configured-Assemblage is a developmental landmark proposal composed of reconfigured traces of shipping containers, through diligently reconnecting, revitalizing, and humanizing the accessibility of the City of Long Beach, Long Beach Blvd and the Broadway area. Through proposing three types of innovatively reconstructed modular shipping containers, the overall construct leads to open courtyards, interlocking units, and playfully generated programs that introduce a new innovative topological design that regenerates and reconnects the community.

Bringing together a fusion of technological, economical and cultural entities, and combining a public free space into an interlocked modular construct, which includes an internal courtyard as public landscape, the newly developed (RE)Configured-Assemblage becomes an open playground of hidden gems, which offers the community countless integrated opportunities to develop and harmonize the City of Long Beach, and the Long Beach Blvd area. The shifting of the vertical containers on the Intelligent Daylight Façade represents the constant movement of containers in the nation's busiest container port.

(RE)Configured- Assemblage acts as an intermediary "connector" and "infiltrator" within five main connections of interlocked programmatic organization: Institutional (Eco-Edu Centre), Studios/Art Galleries/Loft Spaces (which also act as temporary lodging spaces), Commercial (Retail/Stores), and two F&B options (Cafe Ground Floor/Roof Top Bar). It challenges the visceral and abundantly urbanized City of Long Beach, and the Long Beach Blvd area that sustainability feeds itself through both land and sun.

Through building a new and innovative infrastructural system that feeds into the 'connectors', each layer of program interlocks and intersects each other, by regenerating new energy and systematic advances it creates continued developmental and renewed energy along each path.

Collaboration: WE-DESIGNS.ORG, XP& Architecture
Project lead: Wendy W Fok, Judith Mussel
Design architect: Wendy W Fok
Project architect: Judith Mussel
Design team: Ben Vongvanij, Barnett Chaunault, Rolando Lopez
Cost estimator: Jenny Chow / Judith Mussel
Technical / Environmental Consultant: Judith Mussel, LEED AP / Jenny Chow, LEED AP
Location: Long Beach, California, USA

The Unrolled/Reconfigured Container Skin is a secondary 'skin'. Made entirely from access and unfolded containers it compensates for the Southern California Climate, acting to protect the interior containers from extensive solar heat gain. The secondary skin saves on cooling compensation measures like HVAC systems or expensive insulation materials, while offering an in-between. Additionally, the secondary skin and internal containers mediate as a threshold for natural ventilation that exhausts the remaining excessive heat gain. Alternately, the Intelligent Daylight Façade development of (RE) Configured- Assemblage, through the arrangement of a "O" ring plan typology, offers both adaptive space planning (creating ad-hoc creative and dynamic spaces for exhibition and open-use), and spacious circulation from the East and West wings of the building. While the technology of the façade, designed with sequential openings of the corrugated container skin and Bio-Glass elements, provides punctures for additional ventilation and solar louvers which provides sufficient daylight for its occupants on higher level floors.

Understanding that in Southern California many indoor tasks can be performed outside, the "O" ring Dynamic Space Controlled Circulation Façade acts dualistically as a threshold and intermediary space, between the core occupiable spaces and circulatory spaces. Through the geometrical manipulation of containers (the vertical pushing or pulling of the containers) against each other, (RE)Configured- Assemblage creates outdoor spaces (balconies) that act as additional space to be utilized by occupants. Open air areas are also protected from exposure by either the secondary skin or green-roof.

An added touch is the Readapted Containers as Furniture/Planters, which circulate the edge of the building on the ground floor. These Street Furniture and Planters—designed in three scales of 1ft (glass patches), 3ft (flower planters), 5ft (seating/lighting/shrubbery)—are means of incorporating reconfigured containers as street seating, rest areas for occupants and visitors, while providing street lighting for the building itself.

Modular: planter / seating / street lighting units
total containers for terrain: 18 units

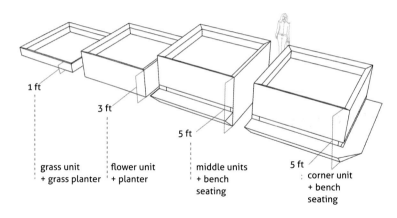

1 ft	3 ft	5 ft	5 ft
grass unit + grass planter	flower unit + planter	middle units + bench seating	corner unit + bench seating

Container sizing chart: façade / central space units
total containers for central space: 96 units
total containers for façade: 64 units

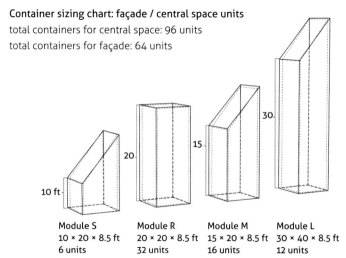

Module S	Module R	Module M	Module L
10 × 20 × 8.5 ft	20 × 20 × 8.5 ft	15 × 20 × 8.5 ft	30 × 40 × 8.5 ft
6 units	32 units	16 units	12 units

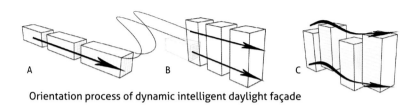

Orientation process of dynamic intelligent daylight façade

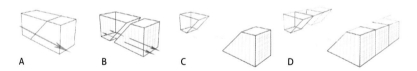

Process of creating the edge condition

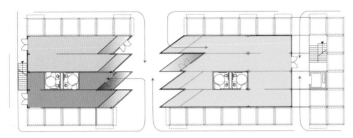

Ground floor plan

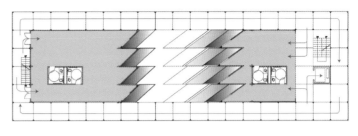

Roof plan

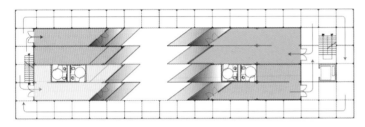

2nd floor plan

Roof top cafe
S - studio lofts
M - studios
L - lofts
Retail cafe
Eco-edu center
Green space
→ Pedestrian access

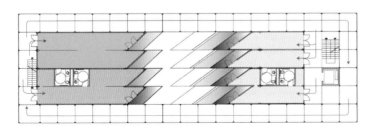

3rd floor plan

4th floor plan

South elevation

North elevation

1. Structural metal frame of containers
2. W 12 × 30
3. Corrugated metal sheet of container, punctured holes and louvers for illumination
4. Bio-glass sliding doors
5. Certified wood decking
6. Rigid insulation
7. Original container floor and roof build-up
8. Batt insulatiom

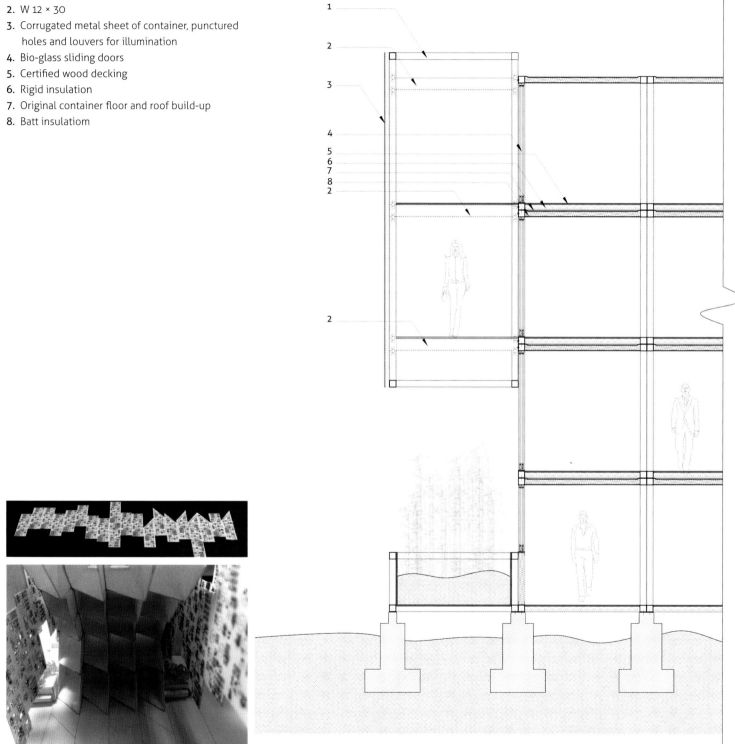

Wendy W Fok | WE-DESIGNS.ORG

Urban Weave

Urban Weave is a developmental master planning proposal which traces through humanizing the accessibility of the Georgia and Dunsmuir viaducts and Northeast False Creek Waterfront development area, through proposing new branching open landscapes and the bifurcation of programmes, which introduces innovative topological energy creation that regenerates and reconnects the community.

Acting as an intermediary "connector", "weave", and "infiltrator" within four main strands of intertwined organization—Ecology, Pedestrian, Vehicular, and Infrastructure— Urban Weave challenges the visceral and abundantly urbanized Georgia and Dunsmuir viaducts and proposed waterfront developmental area that feeds itself through both land (piezoelectric) and water (sea & storm water retention system).

Urban Weave is composed of modular and interwoven strips on an urban scale. It starts as a surface sectioning off into multiple layers. By manipulating the layers with operations like perforation, triangulation, bifurcation, and punctuation, urban landscapes and spaces are created which could house various functions and needs. The individual modular strips are interwoven to form a park that is fluid and ongoing, whereby each layer of program weaves and intersects each other and generates new energy.

The straps are not only landscapes but also an innovative idea combining nature, leisure/function and sustainability. These multilayered developments offer a plethora of opportunities, microclimates, and developmental programs. On the top layer natural landscapes provide citizens with a breath of fresh air. The straps provide different microclimates to help adjust the city's environment and temperature while sustaining themselves with little need for outside maintenance.

Studio: WE-DESIGNS.ORG
Design lead: Wendy W Fok
Design team: Jose Aguilar, Pratik Eamon
Project team: Ben Vongvanij, Rolando Lopez, Carolyn Glenn, Kimberley McGrath
LEED AP: Jenny Chow
Projected project year: 2012 (Phase I) / 2015 (Phase II)
Competition: reCONNECT - Visualizing the Viaducts
Location: Vancouver, BC, Canada (Georgia/Dunsmuir Viaducts & Northeast False Creek Waterfront Development)

The park would be zoned into different themed areas, with different programs and event venues inserted into the straps. The linear arrangement of the ecological straps creates maximum edges for different interactions between the ecological zones and the programs. Human activities and nature combine easily in circulation spaces that criss-cross the landscape, up and down, in and out.

A pioneering a storm water retention zone and H2O desalination technology are located below and between the general area of the Georgia and Dunsmuir viaducts at the deepest levels of the infrastructure layer of the bifurcating ecological landscape. Here a high-powered desalination plant is housed, which functions to collect and purify the water of False Creek Bay. There is enough to introduce new programs that involve a water park and an open-air playground, but also potentially to become an economic leader in recycling the grey water, a system which could hydrate the plantations and urban farms within the Greater Vancouver Area, and to provide Vancouverites with an additional 20% of drinking water. Bringing together a fusion of technological, economical and cultural entities, and combining a public free space into an interwoven landscape, the newly developed Urban Weave becomes an open playground of hidden gems, which offers the community countless integrated opportunities to develop and harmonize the Georgia and Dunsmuir viaducts area and the newly developed Northeast False Creek Waterfront District.

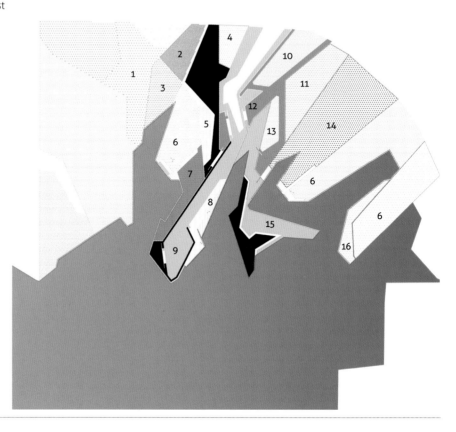

1. Bird concert
2. Douglas firs
3. Oregon oaks
4. Cherry blossoms
5. Restaurant
6. Boat dock
7. Public plaza
8. Ramp to seawalk
9. Observation deck
10. Willow trees
11. Pacific dogwood trees
12. Trail
13. Grass area
14. Open concert area
15. Sea walk
16. Sand beach

1. Recreation / private commercial
2. Civic / public / museums
3. Transportation hub
4. Urban farm stations
5. Program
6. Circulation
7. Water retention
8. Farmland
9. Landscape / grass
10. Pedestrian pathways
11. Skytrain
12. Dunsmair and Georgia viaducts

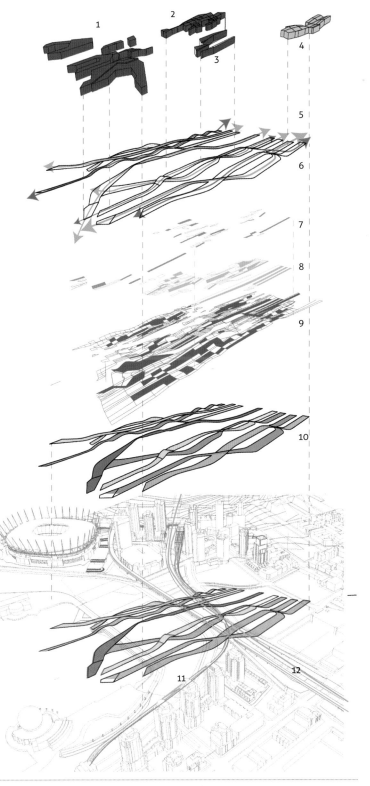

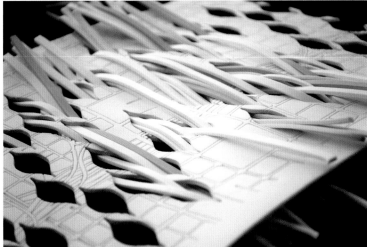

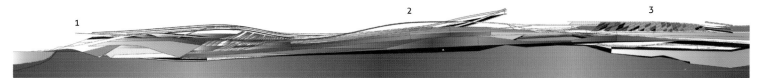

Three main sources of recycled energy are brought into the site to extend its energy for better use:

Retrofitting the Urban Viaduct through Piezoelectric Generators: (TBA)

Regenerated Water Energy: Pioneering a storm water retention zone and H2O Desalination technology below and between the general area of the Georgia and Dunsmuir viaducts area at the deepest levels of the infrastructure layer of the bifurcating ecological landscape, houses a high-powered desalination plant, which functions to collect and purify the water of False Creek Bay. There is enough to introduce new programs that involve a water park and open-air playground, but also to recycle grey water and potentially hydrate plantations and urban farms, as well as providing Vancouverites with 20% more drinking water.

H_2O Technology:
+ reverse osmosis - using liquid sewage and making potable H2O
+ desalination - recycling sea water to brown/grey water for agriculture
+ storm water retention for recreation, water art installations, and sculptures.

Acoustic Cooling through collected extraneous noise: Sound Cooling is the newest of all technologies which the current US military is utilizing for refrigeration and chilling systems. Through a "Sound Strip" collection of at least 190db of sound through the highway between the Georgia and Dunsmuir viaducts and adjacent neighbourhoods. A sound tunnel would be contructed through the Vehicular layer of the bifurcation, acoustic energy (similar to piezoelectric energy) could regenerate enough to power 60% of the homes in the new False Creek Waterfront area—while also providing refrigeration and cooling for the Skytrain station next to the new waterfront area, which houses a new shopping mall, library, concert hall, and community centre.

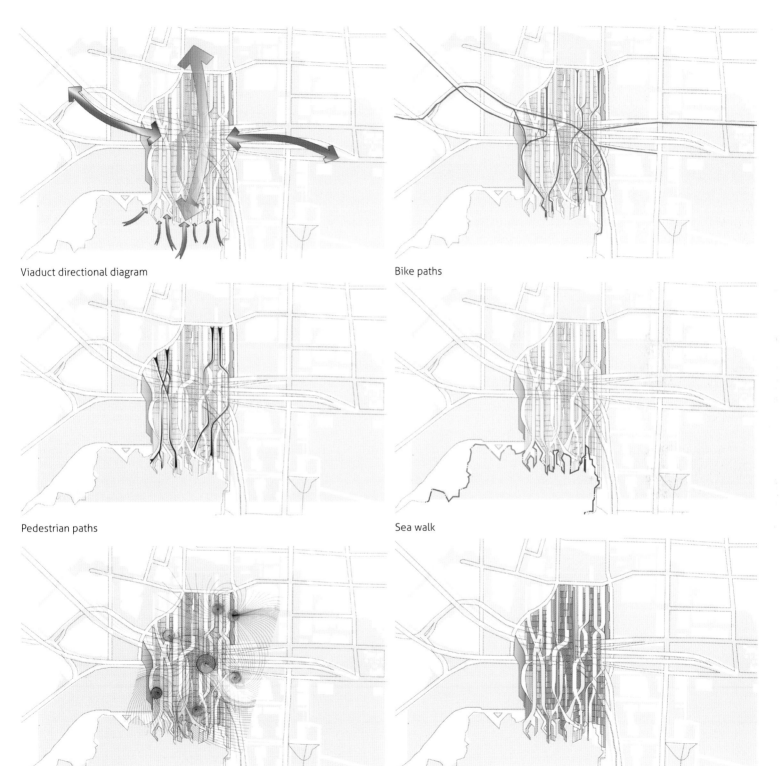

Viaduct directional diagram

Bike paths

Pedestrian paths

Sea walk

Programmatic diagram

Green space diagram

Gage / Clemenceau Architects

Khaosiung Pop Center

The Khaosiung Pop Center is the first building proposal to integrate the solarpod technology into the building envelope. By fusing larger massing containers that shelter a performance space and its auxiliary spaces, the building exists as a single entity at the levels where the program is distributed. Farther up, as the mass dissolves into a series of open peaks, each container reasserts its individual identity and provides housing for a robotically activated solar collection system. The system deploys in peak solar conditions, and retracts to better shelter the high-performance solar technology within each pod.

Either freestanding or integrated into new or existing buildings, solarpods are a robotically automated building accessory that deploy only at times of peak solar efficiency. The pods extend from within the building, and unfurl to reveal climatically fragile, yet hyper-efficient solar cells to collect building energy. The solarpod shell, when retracted and closed, protects the fragile high-yield solar technology when no sunlight is available, and when activated, maximizes exposure of these cells to the sun through robotic movement. This action additionally provides a visual aesthetic experience that calls attention not only to the building, but the act of energy retrieval. The solarpod allows cities to resist the application of only aesthetically inert technical solar cladding, in favor of a system that is strategic, educational, focused and offers an everyday spectacle and reminder of the expenditure and retrieval of energy. The reflective qualities of the solarpods are generated using a prototype parametric rendering system that links surface geometries to lighting sources and intensities. By adjusting the lighting qualities, the forms can be updated to best reflect sunlight and their surroundings to cast shadows and reflections on specific locations.

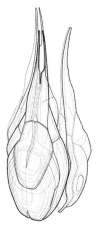
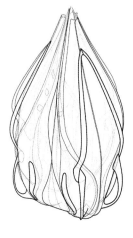

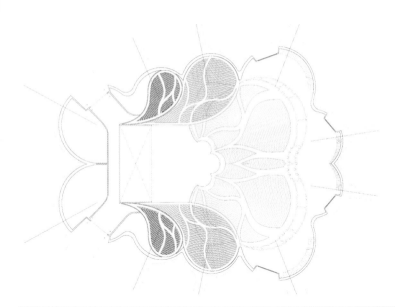

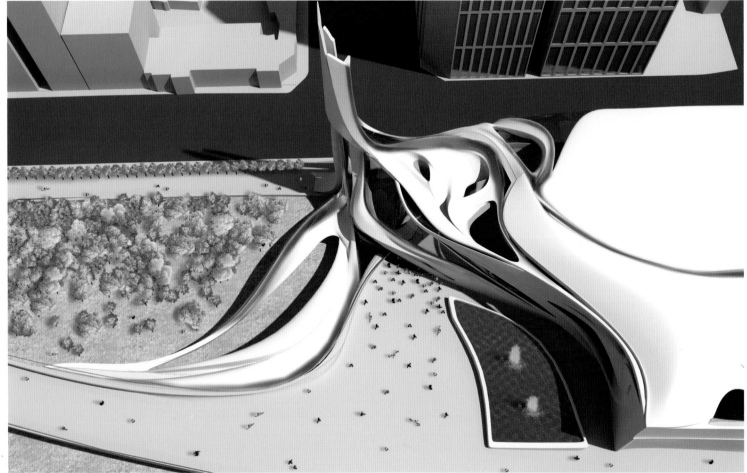

Lorene Faure & Kenny Kinugasa-Tsui / Horhizon

Archifoliage Veils

The rapid development of innovative technological approaches in the realm of biology, biomechanics, biotechnology, aerodynamics, and hydrodynamics are becoming of immense significance to architecture, demanding our attention due to their inevitable cultural, aesthetic and technical implications. This results in the 'biologicalization' phenomenon in architecture. The line between the natural and the artificial is progressively blurred.

Based on the research into plant flowers fertilization and fermentation mechanisms, the proposed artificial synthetic structures create a family of responsive and interrelated typological growth structures to nurture specific crop plants living systems.

The biological phenomena in morphological terms have been studied and principles applied as a means to develop new structural and formal systems. The designed synthetic archifoliage veil structures are each tailored to nurture different species of living crop to grow symbiotically in an optimized condition.

The images on the right record the growth pattern for a climbing plant on the archifoliage system. The resultant geometry of the vegetation is generated from the differentiated nurturing forms of the archifoliage veil structures. The vegetation forms a soft outer skin for the building, which changes seasonally according to the annual growth and cultivation of the farm.

The design of the archifoliage Veils system researched fluid dynamics as the conceptual and technical basis for choreographing complex interactions of crop growth from computationally generated vector fields. The ecological environmental data such as sunlight, temperature and rain is incorporated into the iterative design progression of the veils family typologies.

The research has been applied in two urban agriculture proposals, the Beer Hops Farm Brewerymarket and the Hybridized Farm Bridge as a City Garden.

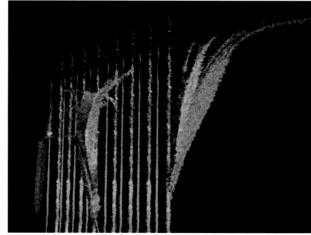

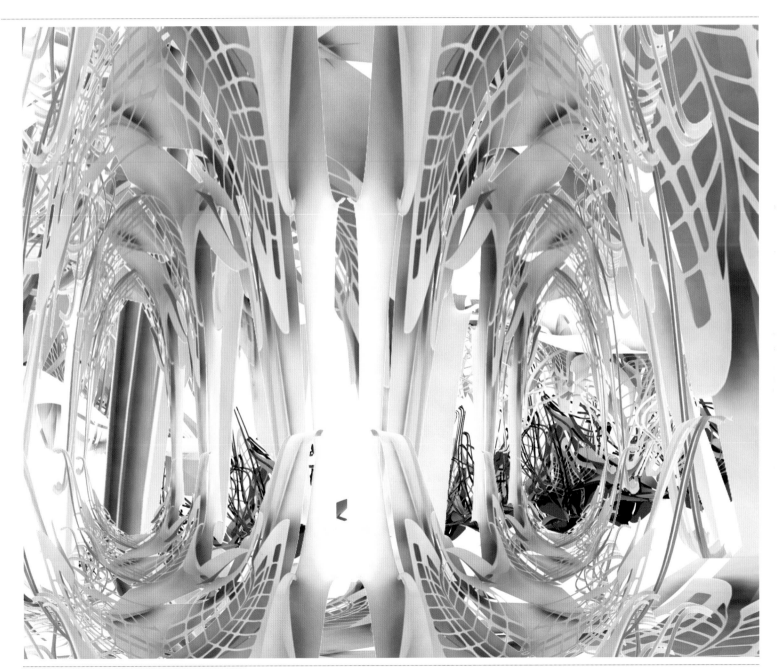

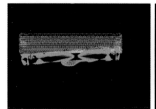
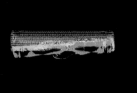
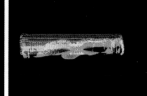

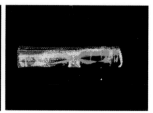

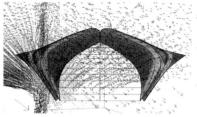

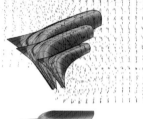

Archi-zantedeschia elliottiana - beans

Archi-zantedeschia aethiopica - gourd

Archi-zantedeschia rehmannii - cucumbers

Archi-zantedeschia albomaculata - yam

Archi-zantedeschia jucunda - squashes, tomatoes, salads and herbs

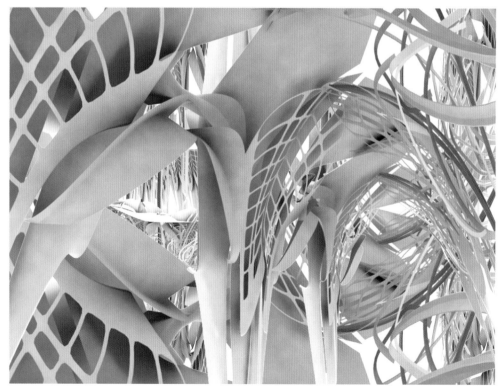

Araceae is a family of monocotyledonous flowering plants in which flowers are borne on a type of inflorescence called a spadix. The spadix is usually accompanied by, and sometimes partially enclosed in a leaf-like hood.

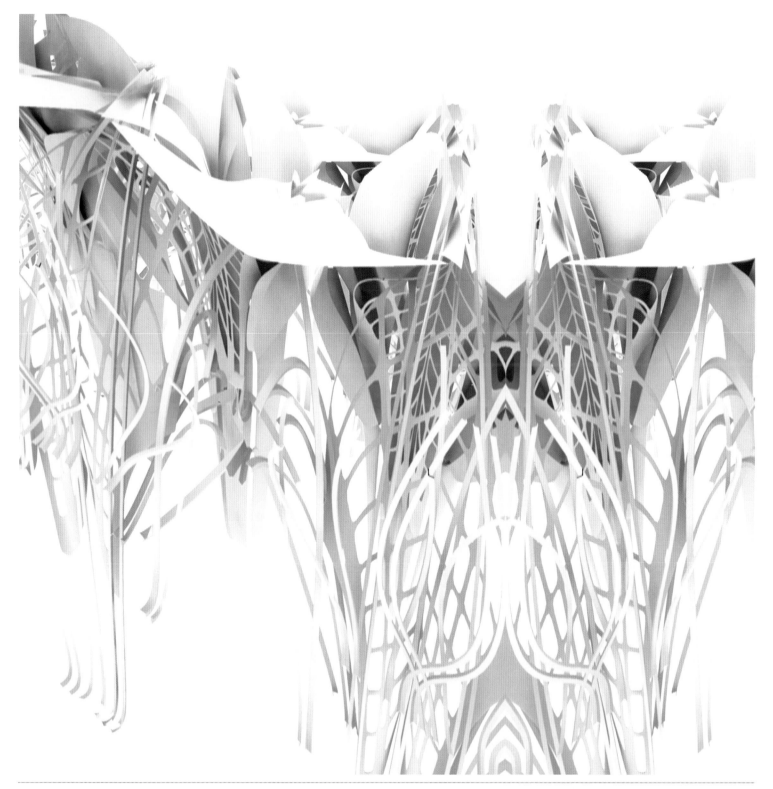

Research application 1:
Urban Agriculture. Beer Hops Farm Brewerymarket

This urban agricultural proposal is a 'Beer Hops Farm Brewerymarket' that aims to create a new place for the exchange of goods and service in the historic Highland Square district of West Highlands neighborhood. The Brewerymarket's main entrance is on West 32 Avenue, enroute to Downtown Denver where the annual American Beer Festival at the Colorado Convention Center is held. The building acts as a 'reception' to the global events of Denver and strengthens West Highland neighborhood's local identity through an innovative year round programming including hop plant farm-

ing, beer making, and providing flexible vending market spaces with a community events venue for arts and music performances. Hop plant (Humulus Lupulus) is vigorous climbing vegetation and hops are used primarily as an important flavoring and stability agent in the beer making process. The proposal creates the sensual experience of a vibrant 'garden' where the hops are farmed on hop poles to create the building's main green facade. The adjustable assembly systems of the modular vending bins are inspired from the natural material properties of hop pods.

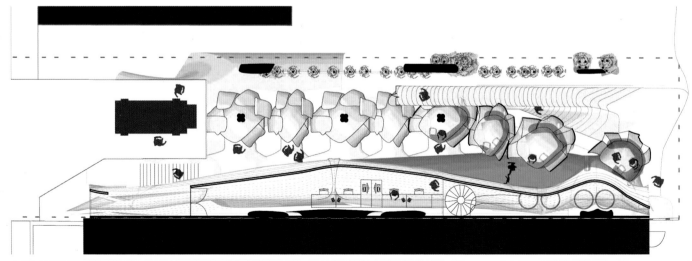

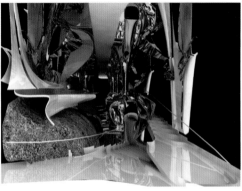

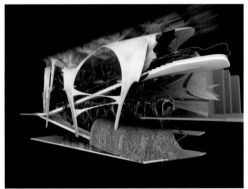

Research application 2:
Urban Agriculture- Biosynthetic Ecology: Hybridized Farm Bridge as a City Garden

Most cities in the world rely on a vulnerable system of food supply; hence they are most likely to feel the effects of any food shortages. In the UK, it is estimated that Londoners consumed 6.9 million tones of food per year, of which 81% came from outside the UK. The country's food supply is almost totally dependent on oil (95% of the food we eat is oil-dependent) and if the oil supply to Britain were suddenly cut off, figures show that it would take just three full days before law and order broke down. (Sources from London Yields: Urban Agriculture. An exhibition held at the Building Centre, London during 9 April - 30 May 2009)

The transformation of cities from consumers of food to generators of agricultural products not only increases food security but also contributes to sustainability, improved health and poverty alleviation.

This has driven an in-depth research based investigation into the proposition of an urban agricultural building hybridized with biological matter, as a semi-living system that informs a biosynthetic ecology that would provide food for Londoners.

The architectural proposal is a technological food production farm built on top of the existing Westminster Bridge in central London. A system of an archifoliage 'veils' allows a variable input from the surrounding natural habitat and human influence into a public garden spectacle, while preserving its original function as a road bridge. The veils morphologically adapts to the existing stone bridge and forms a number of floating docks on the Thames River that accommodates the function of food delivery through water vehicles, as well as leisure activities such as canoeing and kayaking.

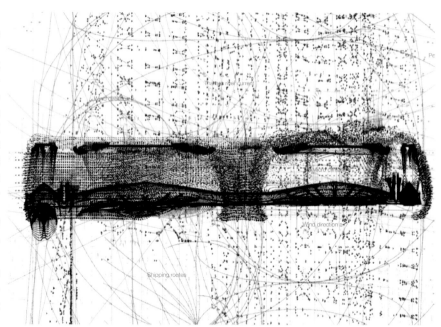

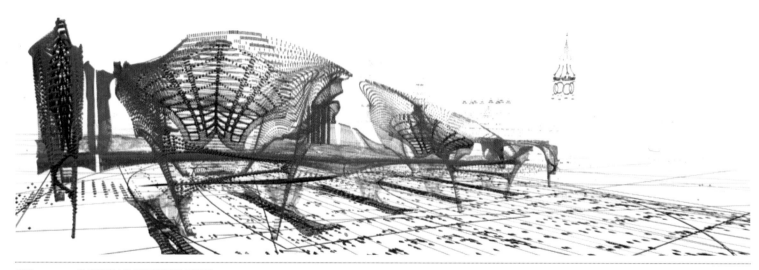

Jaenes Bong – Jonathan Alotto

Phyto-Depuration Towers

The Phyto-Depuration Towers are located in a suburb on the North of Paris periphery ring. They are ecological towers designed for collecting and recycling the rain water, with the purpose of reducing water consumption in daily life. The design is inspired by the lotus plant. The lotus has a large leaf-like water receiver and stands on its very thin stem. The form-finding process was to test different types of lotus leaf shape in order to derive the most dynamic result in response to its constraint. The branching system supports the leaf in all circumstances, and the water filtration system, also known as Phyto-Depuration system, is applied like multiple waterfalls in order to convert rain water to usable water.

To analyze the water consumption statistic, the 10,000 sqm (32,808 sqft) grid has been introduced onto the location plan. The number of houses and apartments define the approximate number of people, which is then defines the water consumption. The center of the grid is the fixing point of the towers position. The generation of the sizes and positions is systematically parametric. As much relevant data as possible is collected as inputs, to respond to the need, as output.

Design: Jaenes Bong – Jonathan Alotto
Location: Paris, France

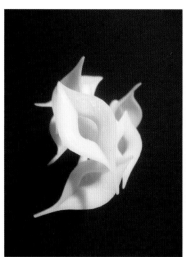

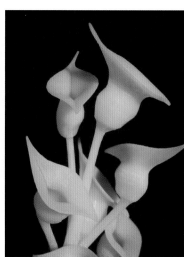

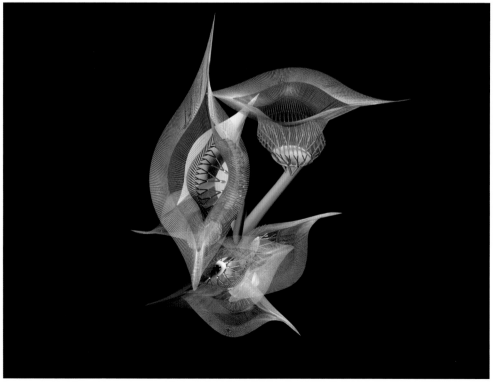

Right: Wind tunnel diagram study for form-finding process.

This process allows us to test different shapes to study the wind turbulance they create. The sudy is inspired by the two types of lotus leaf, the leaf of the lotus that grows in lakes and the leaf of the lotus that grows by the sea. The sea lotus has to face stronger winds and has adapted its leaf shape to create less wind turbulance.

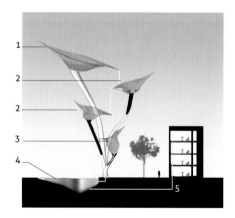

1. Rainwater receiver
2. Purification passage
3. Purified water process
4. Water storage / pond
5. Water distribution

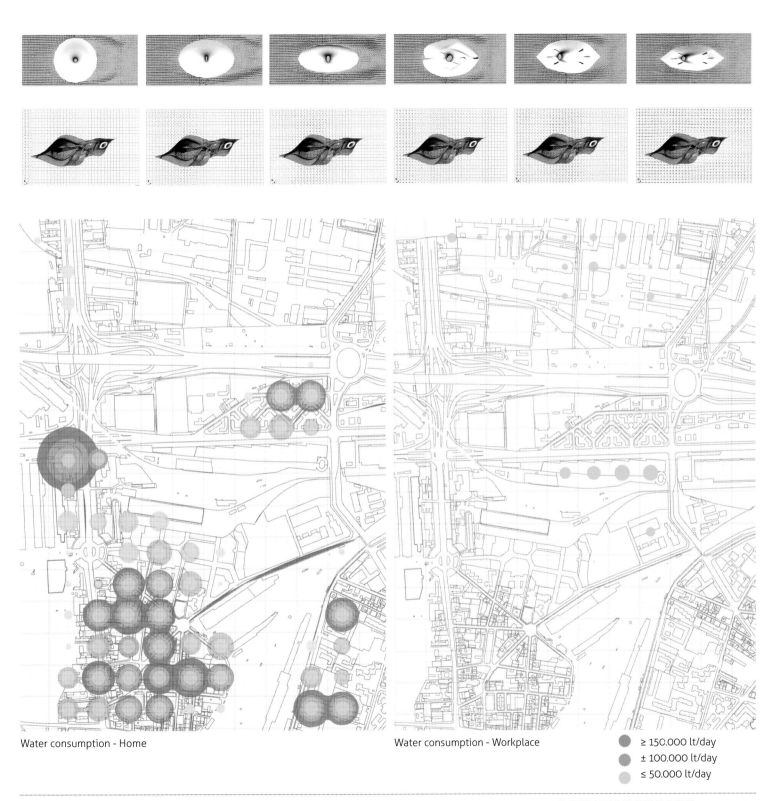

Water consumption - Home

Water consumption - Workplace

≥ 150.000 lt/day

± 100.000 lt/day

≤ 50.000 lt/day

SDA

New Taipei City Art Museum

The New Taipei City Art Museum is conceived as the architectural expression of a dynamic and fluid lifestyle/art experience. It is not only a museum of contemporary art; it is an architectural and civic landmark that shapes the visual and spatial experience of the visitors to the museum, the users of the park it inhabits, and the citizens of the city it represents. It is a dynamic building that is inherently connected to the identity of New Taipei City, and furthermore augments that identity through its iconic presence.

The design of the museum challenges the conventional notion of a museum as a centralized network of enclosed galleries each to be experienced in serial fashion, but instead proposes a gradient network of continuously connected and articulated spaces with no start and no end. The programs of both the Contemporary Art Museum and the Children's Museum are arranged as closed loops of continuous programmatic experience. Each of the loops has been deformed into a three dimensional helicoidal knot which peels away from the ground and cantilevers out to sculpt dramatic interior gallery spaces and define partially enclosed outdoor exhibition spaces. The two knots nest within one another, creating programmatic tangencies articulated by peeling transitions and surfaces where they overlap, thus opening the closed condition of the two loops into a single continuous spatial network.

Design: SDA | Synthesis Design + Architecture
Location: New Taipei City, Taiwan
Date: 2011

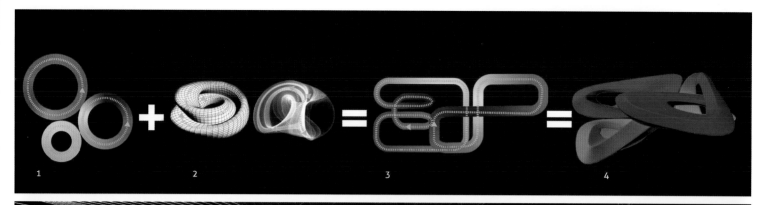

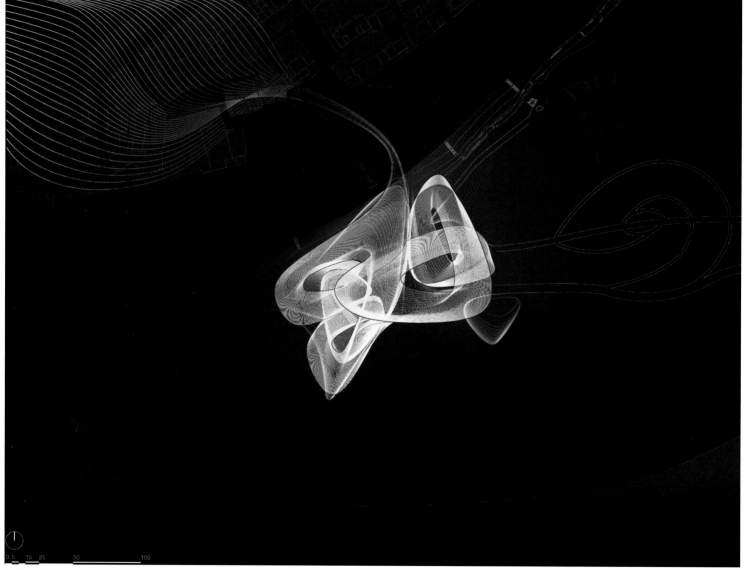

1. Looping program gradient
2. Geometric operation (helicoid and Clein Bottle)
3. Circulation and program gradient diagram
4. Program gradient applied to final geometry

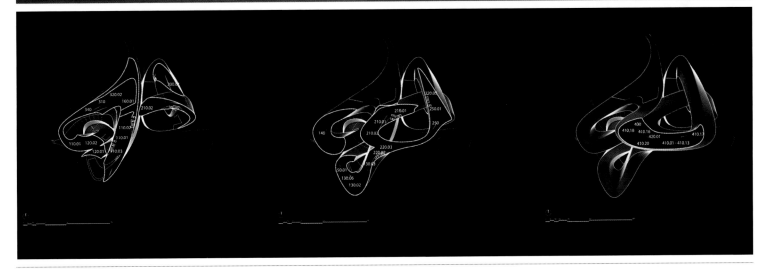

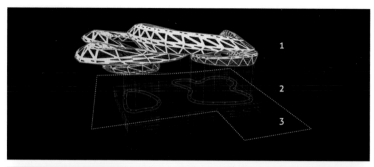

Structure diagram

1. Tubular steel space frame
2. Concrete beam
3. Concrete pile foundation

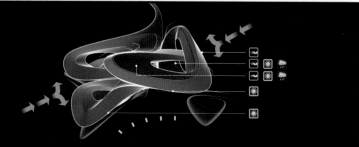

Passive sustainability

Prevailing winds from NE

Microclimates in protected courtyards:

- Wind protection
- Solar protection
- Rain water collection
- Natural ventilation

North facing roof:

- Indirect daylighting

South facing cantilever:

- Solar protection
- Rain shelter

South facing roof:

- Solar protection

Exploded axonometric

1. Tubular steel space frame
2. Glazed ceramic louvre system
3. Sky bridge to Yinnke Station
4. Permanent galleries
5. Temporary galleries
6. Special exhibition spaces
7. Outdoor exhibition spaces
8. Lobby
9. Libraries
10. Lecture hall
11. Shops

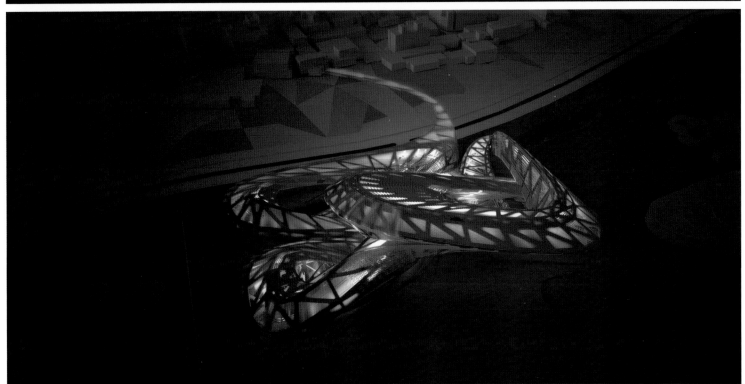

upgrade.studio [Oana Maria Nituica & Claudiu Barsan-Pipu]

NYMPHA Cultural Center - urban bioHybrid

Urban bio-hybrid is one of the results of an urban research platform developed by the upgrade.studio office in Bucharest. The research emphasized a new way of urban development by analyzing urban tissue and the way it has been generated so far. The designers consider that each city has emerged differently with its own genetic characteristics encoded in the urban tissue. Building-up a new future with no reference to this matter, in the context of architectural globalization where any new building could fit in almost any place in the world, could harm our cultural expression.

The research implied an urban tissue "scan" with the help of a software (developed in the office) based on mathematical models and algorithms (such as Flocking Theory, Harmonic Search Optimization etc.) Next, a second phase of the research analyzed the urban tissue in terms of dynamics and functionalities underlining the spots where hybrid architecture could be used to re-animate the urban tissue.

At the end of the urban research process the spot-site most requiring an intervention was chosen, and the office designed two hybrids based on the diagrams it had previously obtained.

NYMPHA Cultural Center is a cultural bio-hybrid inspired by the principles of the biological paradigm, a particular architectural species (the architectural hybrid mix of architectural functions being needed in that particular urban tissue) grown into the environment. The bio-hybrid is a morphogenetic reaction to the state of complexity of the environment. It is the result of a number of virtual simulations with parameters measured in the natural environment (wind, sun, temperature, circulations, structure, functional spaces, urban attractors, accessibility and so on). The resulting object is a processed set of information, an architectural endeavor to ease the architect's understanding of the real architectural potential.

The final design of the building following the general morphogenetic approach is also inspired by the biological life, in this case the circulatory system of the leaves and the butterfly chrysalis as a smart reactive skin which protects the inside.

The biologically grown NYMPHA Cultural Center performs like a biological organism reactive to the changing urban context trough a network of veins merged into the body of the building in close relation to a smart skin. This hierarchical system of veins represents the metamorphosis of structure, ducts and passageways in a unifying morphology. The organic property is meant to consistently reduce the energy consumption and the impact the building has on the environment.

Some of the functions of the veins system:

- collecting the pluvial water and recycling it;
- capturing the solar energy and filtering the amount of light that penetrates inside the building;
- cooling and heating the entire body of the building;
- cooling the exterior environment through a mist dispersal system incorporated on the outside face of the vein system;
- storing the water at a medium temperature underground;
- providing flexibility and structural support;
- monitoring the inside and outside environment through sensors embedded into the structure of the veins;
- generating different light intensities during the night in response to the specific functions it comes into contact with.

Internal pipes that irrigate the skin. The intermediate panels are organized to collect rainwater.

The panels have a substructure that absorbs energy through micro-solar panels distributed on the exterior surface.

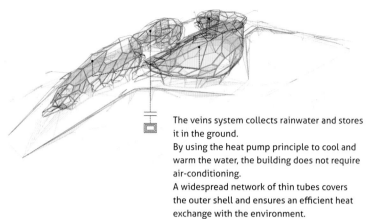

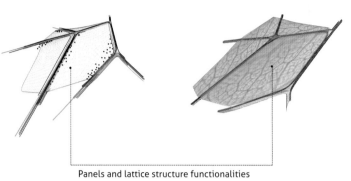

Panels and lattice structure functionalities

The veins system collects rainwater and stores it in the ground.
By using the heat pump principle to cool and warm the water, the building does not require air-conditioning.
A widespread network of thin tubes covers the outer shell and ensures an efficient heat exchange with the environment.

A multiple layer structure system with a mathematical algorithm space distribution.

1. Backstage
2. Foyer
3. Access from parking
4. Bio market
5. Designer shop
6. Storage
7. Exhibition reception point
8. Bar
9. Exhibition
10. Rehersal rooms
11. Stage
12. Administration
13. Cafeteria
14. Meeting room
15. Lounge

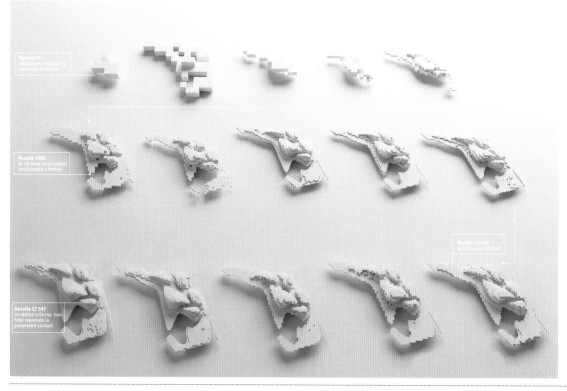

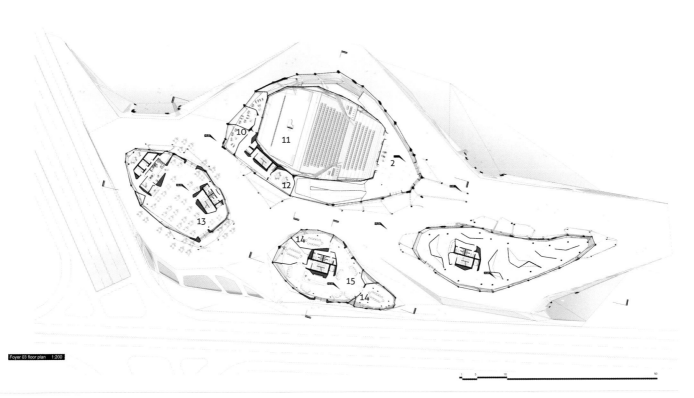

Foyer 03 floor plan   1:200

NYMPHA is the Center for Creative Processes (the name being a metaphor for the analogy with the biological metamorphosis caterpillar-chrysalis-butterfly), hosting a cultural performance hall, conference spaces, workshops for artists and designers, exhibitions, a restaurant/student canteen, a green technological glass house, green market, library, tea house and coffee shop, shops and offices for designers and urban exhibition spaces.

This kind of approach encourages a better relationship with the urban space and the urban tissue, solving some of the biggest problems facing old and the new architectural objects. Using a bottom-up criteria (emergent process) the urban tissue affected by necrosis, inactive or transformed into a "bad neighborhood", could be reanimated and gain a new value.

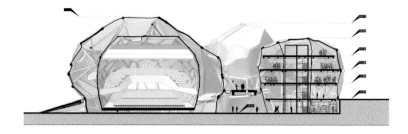

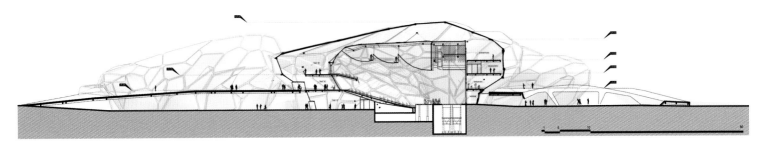

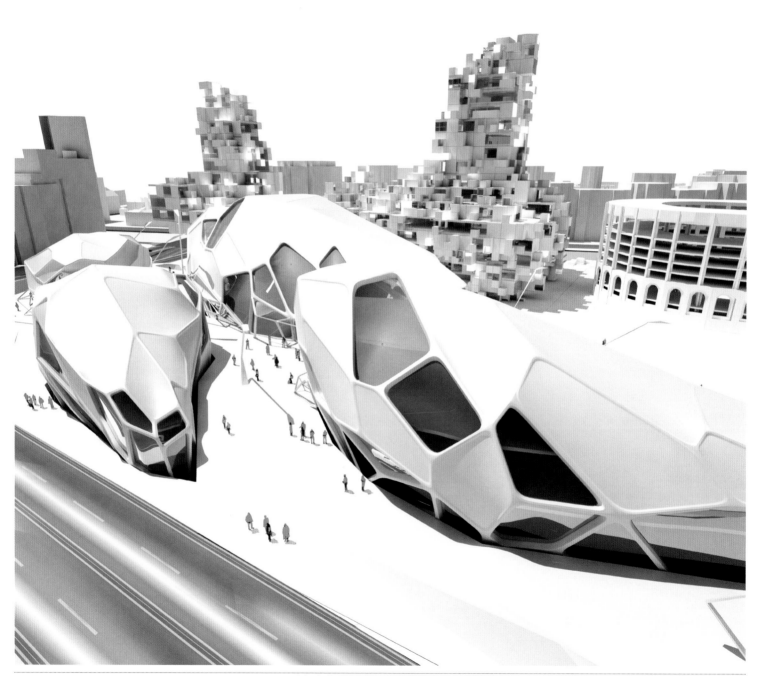

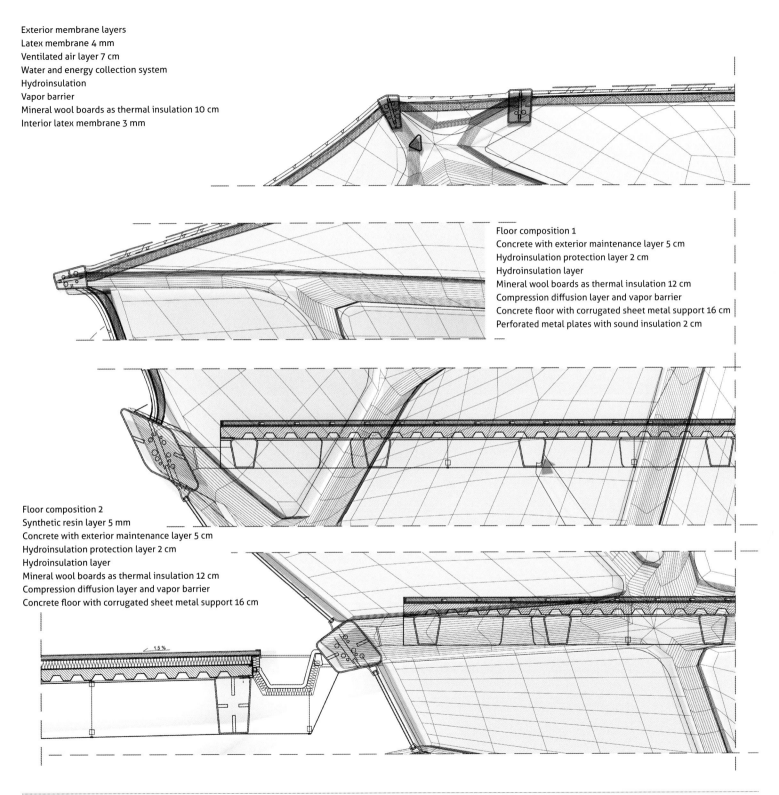

Exterior membrane layers
Latex membrane 4 mm
Ventilated air layer 7 cm
Water and energy collection system
Hydroinsulation
Vapor barrier
Mineral wool boards as thermal insulation 10 cm
Interior latex membrane 3 mm

Floor composition 1
Concrete with exterior maintenance layer 5 cm
Hydroinsulation protection layer 2 cm
Hydroinsulation layer
Mineral wool boards as thermal insulation 12 cm
Compression diffusion layer and vapor barrier
Concrete floor with corrugated sheet metal support 16 cm
Perforated metal plates with sound insulation 2 cm

Floor composition 2
Synthetic resin layer 5 mm
Concrete with exterior maintenance layer 5 cm
Hydroinsulation protection layer 2 cm
Hydroinsulation layer
Mineral wool boards as thermal insulation 12 cm
Compression diffusion layer and vapor barrier
Concrete floor with corrugated sheet metal support 16 cm

Arphenotype

Floating Permaculture

Floating permaculture is a polemical utopian *"system to link systems"* that offers a closed feedback loop of energy and food production. It adapts the futuristic vision of the Metabolist movement of the 1950s and '60s to contemporary society. In this proposal, 'green reactors' are projected onto the shallow waters of the North Sea.

Given the pressure of urbanization on agricultural land in the North Sea's coastal zones, a logical solution would be to generate new farmland on floating islands in order to feed the urban population (more than eighty per cent of our urban areas with a million or more inhabitants are close to an ocean).

As futuristic as all this sounds, the use of floating permacultures is an ancient idea. A thousand years ago the Aztecs used chinampas – floating gardens to feed their cities where normal farmland was barely available. But in this case the floating islands would generate not only food, but energy as well.

The history of civilization can be seen in terms of a competition for food and energy, in which human beings created a distortion in the balance of food and energy chains by taking more out of the system than it could sustain. The development of high-yielding varieties of different crops after World War II, part of the so-called Green Revolution, has boosted food production and helped to reduce the hunger for food. But this was achieved at a high environmental cost, and without reducing the hunger for energy. Quite the opposite, in fact.

An increasing hunger for energy was a driving force behind the development of offshore oil and gas platforms. Offshore platforms could also work to satisfy our hunger for food, using the ideas of the Metabolist movement, which started in Japan in the late 1950s. Metabolism in architecture was based on the idea that the built environment could become an adaptable and expandable megastructure, flexibly responding to changing needs. The Metabolist visions resonated in the work of European architects and artists like Constant and Yona Friedman, who developed utopias housed in comparable megastructures.

Most of these utopian megastructures were concerned with social issues and housing. Food production was hardly a topic, even though the name of the movement suggests otherwise. Few of the projects were related to energy.

Funded by:
The NAI / Jaap Bakema Foundation and A10

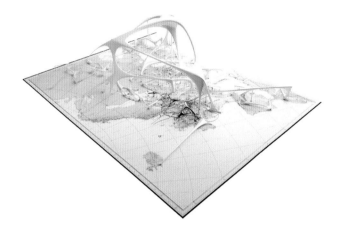

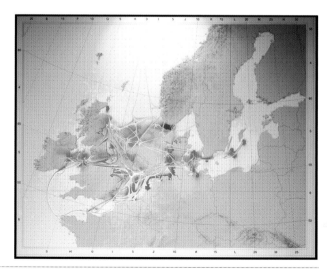

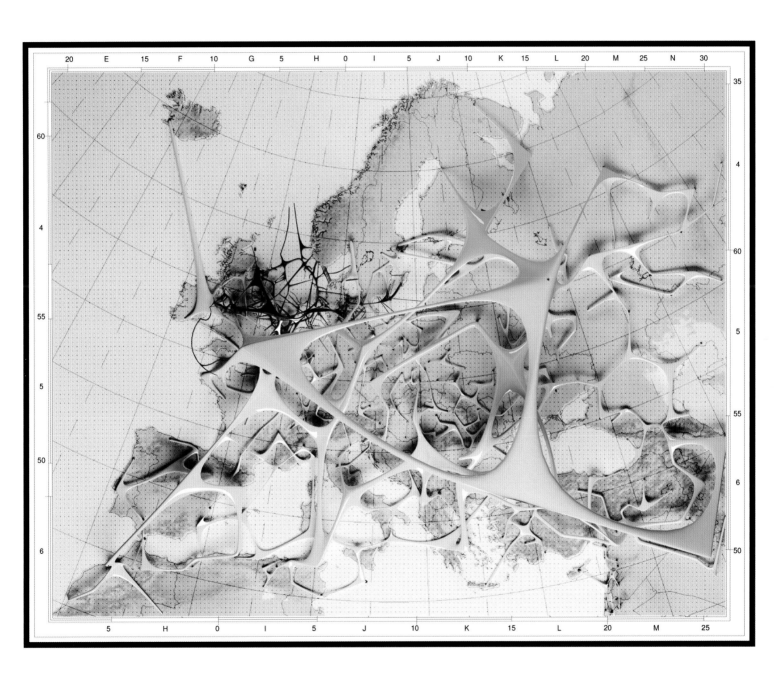

The project blurs the boundaries between floating permacultures and inhabitable megastructures, blending the ideas and visions of the Metabolists with a process of energy and food production that is based on cybernetics, a science developed by Norbert Wiener in roughly the same period as Metabolism.

Cybernetics as described by Wiener deals with 'control and communication between animal and machine', and this opens the way for effectively combining ecology and technology in floating permacultures, creating dynamic balances and eliminating negative feedback loops. Due to the human involvement in the system, it is what von Foerster calls second -order cybernetics. The first order of cybernetics deals with outside observation of the system, while in the second order the observer of the system is part of the system he or she observes. Floating permaculture focuses on second-order cybernetics, because man is always and inevitably a part of the system.

Each permaculture seeks to combine sustainable energy and agriculture in a closed system. The input is divided into natural and waste feeders. Natural feeders gather input from wind and sun resources, while waste feeders gather input from sewage and biomass generated by the megastructures.

We cannot prevent climate change anymore, but we can minimize its effects by acting now by modifying our thinking and through a combination of serious energy efficiency and a wide variety of new technologies. Floating pemaculture as a sophisticated part of a new Metabolism; a positive organism that will adapt to human bodies and culture, creates the battery that will provide the modern autonomous 'Technobody' with energy. Human beings must aim for autarky as a solution to our current over-exploitation of resources.

1st system

1
2
3
4
5
6
7
8
9
10
11
12
13

2nd system

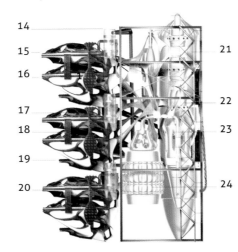

14
15
16
17
18
19
20

21
22
23
24

1. Main reactor
2. Solar receiver
3. Heliostats
4. Algae farm
5. Algae reactor
6. Wind turbines
7. Ventilation
8. Hydroponic gardens
9. Spaceframe structure
10. Compost
11. Wave turbines
12. Enclosure
13. Metal hydride storage

14. Input
15. Vetiver grass 1
16. Vetiver grass 2
17. Zebra mussels
18. Overflow with nutrients
19. Rice pad
20. Chicken
21. Reactor
22. Quench tower
23. Fertilizer
24. Bio oil

Digital Fictions

We have seen in the previous chapters how digital architecture has questioned and redefined important aspects of the architectural object. In many cases the object of an architectural design process is not an unambiguous three-dimensional representation of a building or a constructed building but a process of construction or a set of rules that defines an array of possible forms and articulations. We have also seen how contemporary digital architecture has incorporated and transformed the utopian architectural currents of the 60s.

Another way that digital technologies have affected architecture is in the representational techniques and technologies used by architects. This may seem obvious and simple in relation to other changes but it has its special weight. On the one hand, digital tools have placed the architectural representation inside a matrix of media technologies where it is possible, and sometimes natural, to move away from the traditional architectural representations and turn towards animated images and other technologies. On the other hand, since the object of the design process is no longer a finalized form, architectural drawings may be completely insufficient to transfer the meaning of a design.

In this final chapter we bring together a few projects that illustrate all these influences and issues and stand on the limit of what may be thought as "proper" architecture. Through their subject matter, their medium of expression or both, these projects challenge our ideas and use the tools of contemporary digital architecture to present us with critical and utopian ideas of the future. More than the use of video or their futuristic assumptions these projects are special in that through the influence of digital technologies they have recuperated an idea of architecture as a narrative and as a way of articulating ideas about society and its future.

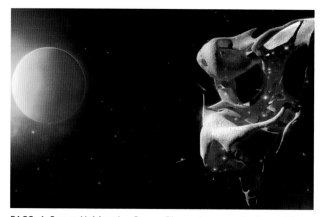

PACC: A Space Habitat by **Sanne Plomp** is an aesthetic and functional representation of the society it houses. Its societal properties -its lack of a currency, the abolishments of any form of government and the absence of any form of power concentration-, together with the day to day activities like sleeping, working, eating and relaxing in a zero gravity environment, created the architecture.

Megalomania, by **Jonathan Gales** of **Factory Fifteen**, is a short animation that explores the aesthetic of change as an ambiguous language that can be read as both growth and decay. The built environment of the city is explored as a labyrinth of architecture that is either unfinished, incomplete or broken. Megalomania is a response to the state of many developing cities, exaggerating the appearance of progress into the sublime. The project took inspiration from Giovanni Battista Piranesi's Carceri plates, which show a fictional architecture of prison environments. The geometry that make up the spaces within the Carceri series is ambiguous of its scale and enclosure and could be argued as impossible to build. These themes were applied to envision an exaggerated contemporary urban construction site on the scale of a city.

Within **Somewhere**, by **Paul Nicholls** of **Factory Fifteen**, we are transported to a time where the boundaries between what is real and what is simulated are blurred. We live online and download places to relax, parks and shopping malls. We can even interact with our friends as if they were in the same room with simulated tele-presence. Everyone is connected and immersed in nanorobotic replications of any kind of object or furnishings, downloadable on credit based systems. Distance and time become as alien as the 'offline'

Stephan Sobl

Vertical Strip – A Hanging Tower

This project is about the interplay of opaque massive surfaces capable of incorporating poché and lightweight, fragile structures. The resulting environments developed by these distinct architectural languages are exploited and distributed vertically to create extreme spatial sequences.

The project is a casino resort, a satellite alternative to Las Vegas, located on a dramatic site between the Hoover Dam and the Bypass Bridge. The resort caters to various 21st century vices including entertainment (concert venues, MMA Fighting), gambling and luxury living. The architectural challenge was taking the conventional vertical tower, including its plinth and orientation, and turning it upside down. The massing layout is construed by the event space on top with a framed view of the Hoover Damm; the casino underneath leading to the hotel lobby and the hotel itself. At the bottom of the tower there is a dramatic area for happenings and ceremonial occasions. It also includes a breakfast room and high end dining with the elevator core floating above the space; a glass floor providing views to the ground; and terraced floor slabs.

In terms of circulation, there are several ways leading into the plinth of the tower, including car circulation; and viewing platforms. The bridge circulation focuses on 3 elements:
- structural details of the Bypass Bridge
- openings to the Hoover Damm
- breathtaking diagonal views of the hanging tower with a constant interplay of plunging and emerging.

Once you arrive at the entrance of the tower, you enter the hanging structure through the supportive strings leading you down through the casino into the hotel lobby.

The structural system is divided into 3 tectonics:
- a massive concrete structure building the cantelivar for the hanging tower
- a lightweight hanging tower
- a metal shell embracing the structure

The tower was generated with a partical simulation based on gravity. In order to achieve structural logic the stings are rotated clockwise and counter-clockwise. The metal shell provides shading and natural wind cicrulation for the tower, whose panels orient themselves according to changing wind conditions.

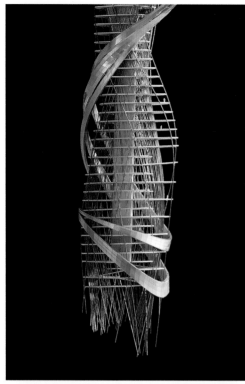

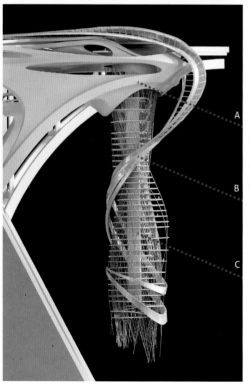

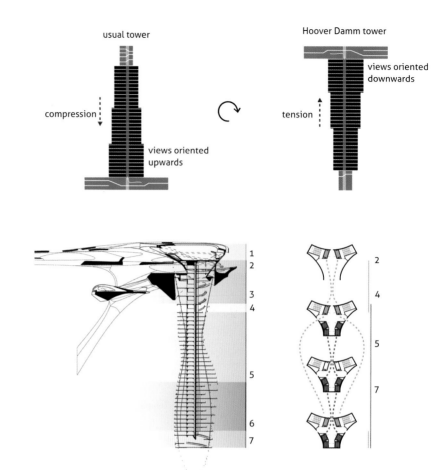

usual tower

compression

views oriented upwards

Hoover Damm tower

tension

views oriented downwards

1
2
3
4
5
6
7

2
4
5
7

A. A massive concrete structure; building the cantilever for the hanging tower
B. A metal shell embracing the structure
C. A lightweight carbon-fiber hanging tower

1. Event space
2. Entrance level
3. Casino
4. Hotel foyer
5. Hotel rooms
6. Luxury suites
7. Hotel event space

Formfinding strategy

The curves are generated with a particle simulation based on gravity.

To achieve a structural logic, a clockwise and counterclockwise rotational field is applied.

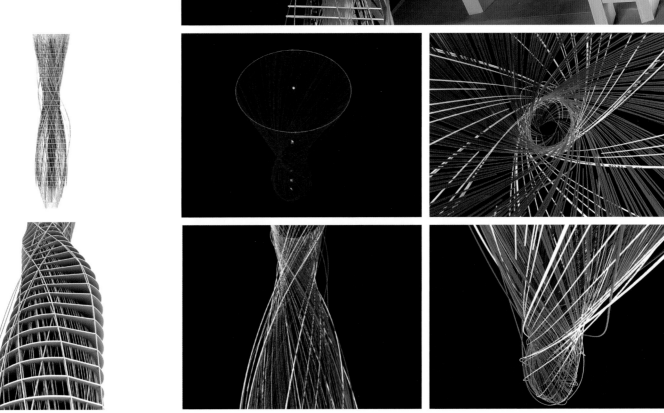

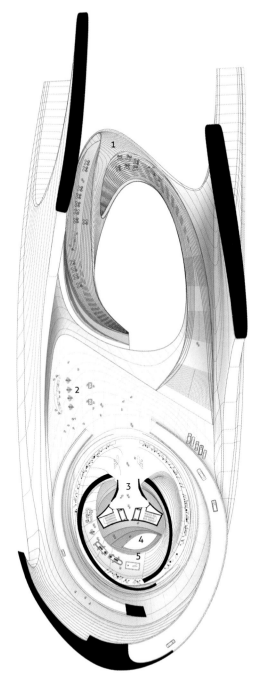

1. Restaurant
2. Lobby
3. Elevator core
4. Casino area
5. Gambling
6. Hotel room
7. Event space
8. Hotel
9. Luxury suite

Lobby level plan

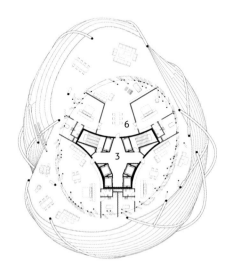

Hotel rooms level plan

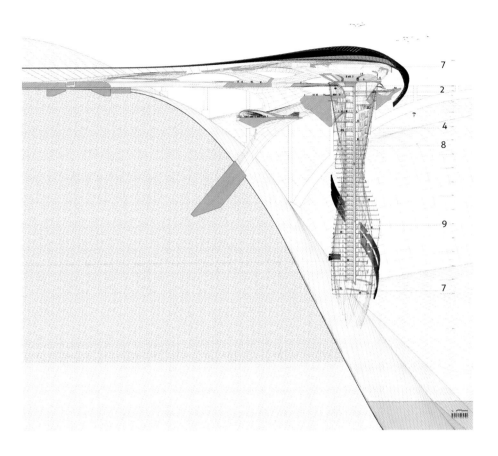

7

2

4

8

9

7

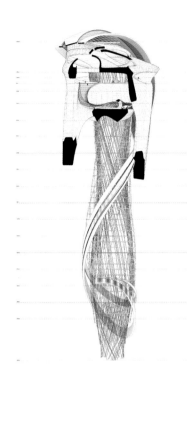

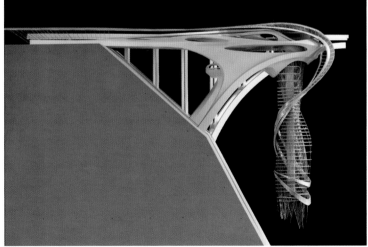

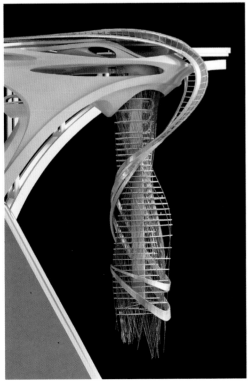

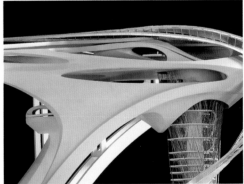

Tuberk Altuntas - Melis Eyuboglu

Bonescraper

The site is in the central business district of Istanbul. On the surrounding plots there were warehouses and factories from the 70's. However, as the city started to expand, the factories moved to the city boundaries and the plots started to host skyscrapers. The plots are connected with the main boulevard. On the side of the plots there are 2-6 story apartments. The empty plot of the project is 22×215m (72x705 ft). The surrounding skyscrapers are up to 261m height.

In this plot boundary, the bonescraper locates itself respecting the surrounding environment. Therefore some restraints are applied to this boundary. These restraints allow the building to escape from the shadow of enormous neighbors and let the light pass through to the buildings around. The porous design also provides structural strength.

The bonelike structure starts to secrete from 3 sources according to these rules. The rules are coded to the DNA of the structure. It passes through phases until it fills the entire boundary. This phasing system allows the owner of the building to construct it in as many phases as they like. This secreting follows the liquid behavior.

The cores are spread through the whole building; they also hold the installations and elements such as stairs. The puffed parts of the structure hold recreation spaces, entrance lobby, social areas, restaurants and sport facilities. The main circulation through the building is maintained through 3D elevators. These elevators are like parasites and move around the façade with their arms. They pick people up from and leave them at the holes on the façade.

The housing units nest on this bonelike structure, and connect to the available slots. These units have different volumes but they all have panoramic views of the city.

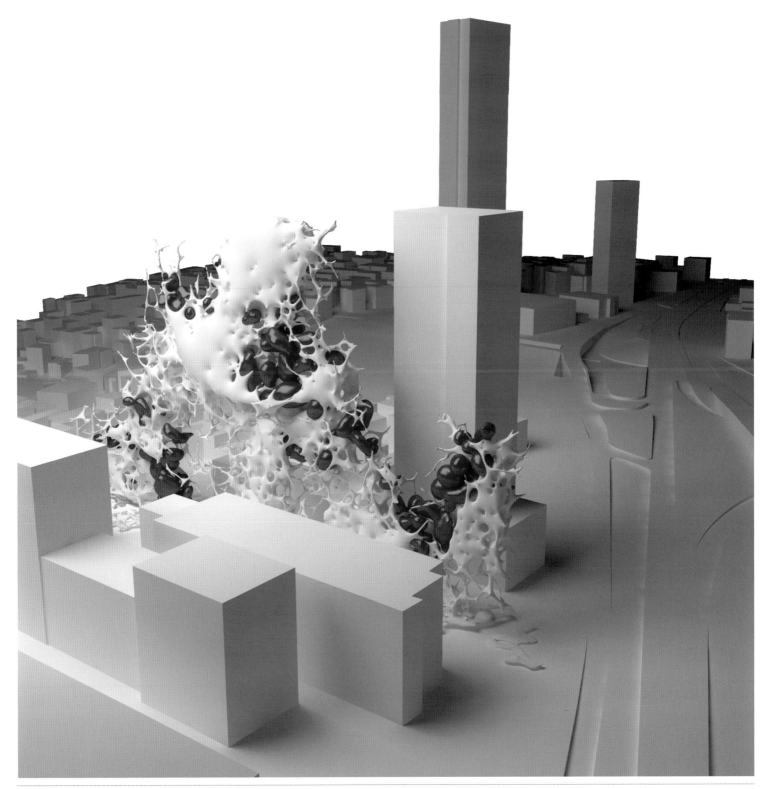

site outline

filled box

volume restraints

production sources

production of bones

surface

<

surface

<

surface

<

surface

nesting of units

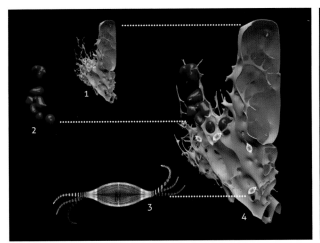

1. Bone-like structure
2. Housing units
3. 3D elevator
4. Structure section

5. Surface close-up
6. Surface material providing transparency

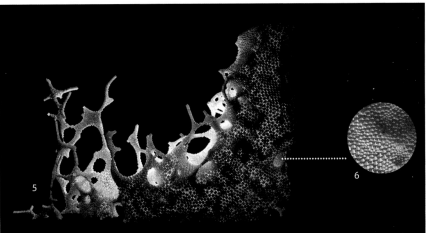

upgrade.studio [Oana Maria Nituica & Claudiu Barsan-Pipu]

stem_space [urban adaptability enhancers]

"Dynamic" is probably the best word to describe a city, yet this particular feature is almost every time bound by a rigid infrastructure that we will henceforth call "the grid". It is precisely this rigid grid dependency of the city that makes it most vulnerable in times of crisis, be it an economic, energetic, social or any other type of menace. Regarding the urbanity as a "species" obeying the evolutionary path [with long periods of stability followed by chaotic phase transitions] we searched for examples of how other complex organisms respond to extreme situations, and found that those which were the most responsive and able to rapidly adapt to fast changing environments survive and maintain their degree of complexity [even thrive], whereas those incapable of coping with their shifting conditions either roll back to a stage of lower complexity or disappear altogether.

The human body is a perfect example of a soft design that owes its current evolutionary complexity to this very capacity of adapting to various extreme scenarios. It does so without undergoing major structural changes, but instead due to the flexibility of the relations present in its systems.

We've focused on a particular element of the human arsenal of responses to crisis situations: stem cells. They have an extraordinary capacity of evolving into virtually any specific type of body cell under both external and internal stimuli of the body, without being pre-programmed, therefore gaining their functions from complex interactions within the system of our body, acting locally, in response to specific "problems" of specific organs or even smaller constituents.

We imagined in this project an architectural equivalent of these stem cells, called the stem_spaces whose role within the city will be that of enhancers of the adaptability that an urban system requires in order to overcome crisis periods by providing the city with the flexibility and self-sufficiency needed in such "transitional" times.

The urban stem cell, the stem_space , is a prefabricated SOFT_SPACE, in the sense that, after being manufactured, its purpose remains undefined and its only "abilities" are those of self-sufficiency [i.e. of providing itself with green, renewable energy, captured by its responsive skin, which can then be stored within its "nucleus"] and of clustering [connecting to other stem_space cells]. The stem_spaces are then distributed throughout the city to different sized communities, and it is the particular LOCAL problems of those communities that will give a functional purpose to each urban stem cell, as, by their interconnection, they can form new urban tissues and even new urban organs as a response to the specific needs of specific groups, allowing the latter to become independent from the rigidity and possible failure/collapse of the GRID.

While human stem cells need to divide, since once specialized, they cannot revert to the stem status, the urban stem_spaces don't require self-division, as, once distributed, they can be "reconfigured" in response to new community demands induced by the crisis situation and to serve new functions within the same tissue or even give birth to completely new urban tissues/organs as needed. Should a community require it, they can be part of a water recycling "urban organ", a solar power-plant, a bio-crop greenhouse, a sanatorium, workshops, etc. with spaces being defined either within each stem_space (such as a hydro or air-phonic mini-farm, a family-size manufacture, small offices, personal healing spaces) or by interconnecting them so as to serve larger urban functions.

Once the crisis period is over, the city would already have made its first steps towards grid independence, by providing an alternative yet equally complex urban system, much more responsive & flexible, that will help it overcome and even prevent future crisis scenarios.

$ Commerce tissue
○ Energy production tissue
✕ Energy production tissue
◎ Food production tissue
✚ Health tissue
ⓘ Information tissue

1. Stem space urban cell: Main components as seen before urban speciation
2. Stem space's responsive skin
3. Stem space's green energy nucleus
4. Stem space matured as habitat space extension
5. Stem space matured as kinetic energy generator
6. Stem space matured as structural system
7. Stem space matured as water collector / recycler
8. Stem space matured as vibrating self-healing space
9. Stem space matured as solar energy harvester

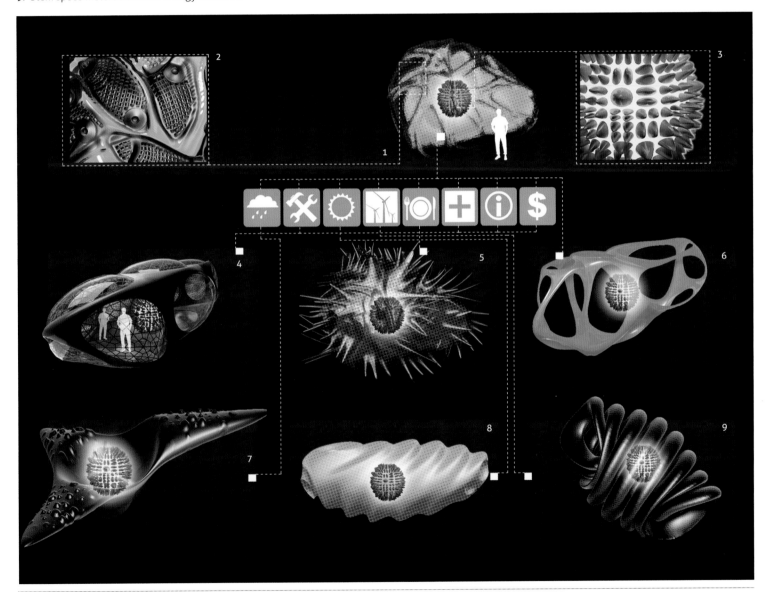

Individual residential tissue sample

Energy producing tissue sample

Collective residential tissue sample

Healing and climatizing tissue sample

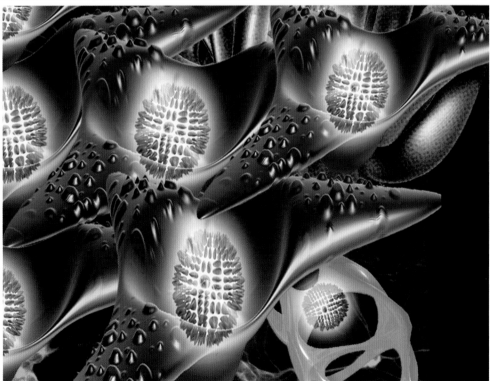

Water recycling tissue sample

Joseph A. Sarafian

Emergent City

By the turn of the twenty-second century, a new epoch in global survival had emerged. The human race was no longer concerned with sustainability as a trend, because it could no longer deny the fact that the world was in fact dying. The environmental catastrophes that surfaced in the twenty-first century became increasingly frequent. Barraged with hurricanes, tornadoes, earthquakes, and tsunamis, mankind was at the brink of extinction.

What emerged was a new strategy in the toolset of disaster housing, but more importantly evolution. Fusing breakthroughs in material science and biology, a band of architects and physicists created a biomechanical organism called the "Arachne". They were designed not only to learn, but to collaborate with humans, fundamentally changing the relationship between man and machine. The Arachne swarm utilizes synthetic muscles derived from the high compression/expansion ratio of carbon nanotubes when they are given an electrical current. The Arachne was engineered to descend upon devastated cities and plug into the city's local information infrastructure. By accessing these "clouds" of information, the Arachne determines site issues of zoning, occupancy fluctuations, and cultural trends. Upon their arrival, the Arachne digs into the decaying earth to extract methane, powering the construction process. The Arachne can not only process traffic patterns, structural loads, and pedestrian hot spots, they collaborate with local residents to build a truly responsive architecture.

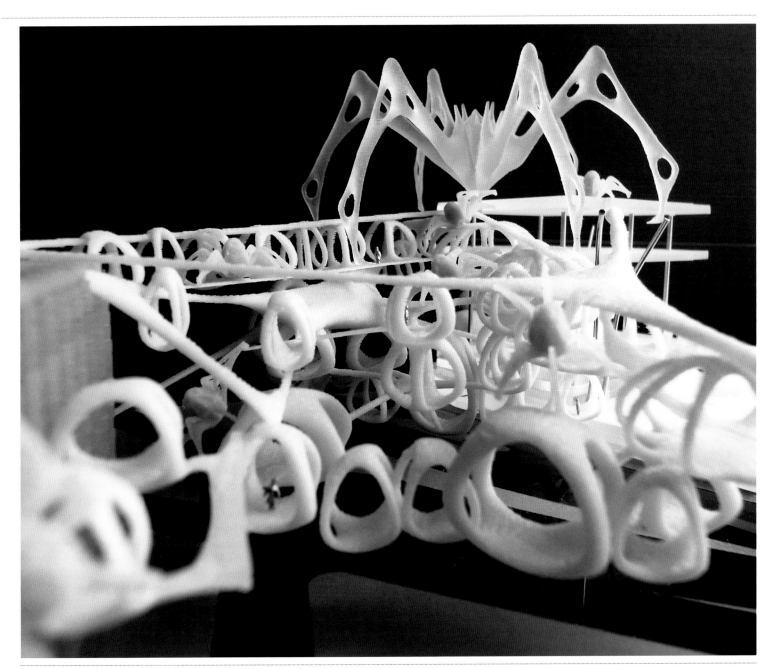

1. Call <Deploy Turbine>
2. Sub <Deploy Turbine>
3. Dim <Release Sequence> = Unclamp propeller
4. Call <Extract Methane>
5. Sub <Extract Methane>
6. Dim <Drill> = Deploy Drill Force (F)=1000psf
7. Dim <Retract Drill> = Initiate Repulsion Force
8. Open <Methane Duct> (P=F/A), A = pipe diameter
9. Activate Pressure Gradient P
10. When Methane=50lb, terminate
11. End Sub

1. Call <Deploy Arachne Swarm>
2. Sub <Deploy Arachne Swarm>
3. Coord. 18° 27′ N, 66° 24′ W
4. Dim <Thrust=X>
5. X(Altitude*Vel) Find Distance (D)
6. If D<20 Then, (Aggregate Swarm)

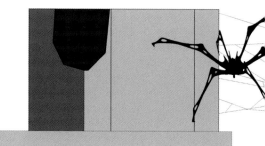

1. Call <Survey Topography>
2. Sub <Survey Topography>
3. Dim <Struct Analysis>
4. Call <Human Program Data: Population Demographics>
5. Call <Spatial Recognition> Coord System: (X,Y,Z)
6. Dim <X> = (LoadPath), Y = (Node Pt)
7. Get Distance, If D = (X*Y) Then, DrawStruct
8. Function: Depth = Span/10
9. Dim <Aggregate Units> Attach Dwellings
10. Call <Sag Deformation Function> L = Dwelling Load
11. End Sub

1. Call <Nested Units>
2. Sub <Nested Units>
3. Dim <Struct Analysis>
4. Call Indigenous Support Struct
5. Call <Spatial Recognition> Coord System: (X,Y,Z)
6. Dim <X> = (LoadPath), Y = (Node Pt)
7. Get Distance, If D = (X*Y) Then, LayerSubstrate
8. Function: Thickness = Height/15
9. Dim <Aggregate Units> Attach Dwellings
10. End Sub

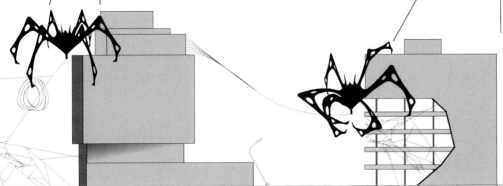

Using the logic of a 3d printer, the Arachne deposit strands of material, including Carbon Nanotubes, Porous Alumina, Nanogel, and Micro-Encapsulated Phase Change Material (MPCM), generating emergent solutions that can be rapidly fabricated with minimal macro-scale details. The Arachne understands two fundamental building types, the suspended unit, and the nested unit. Suspended units are hung from a lattice of spun structure while the nested units are built into existing infrastructure that is salvageable. The structures generated are thus a synthesized byproduct of their environment. The third element that the Arachne creates is the transport bot which is responsible for transporting humans vertically throughout the structure. Residents receive microscopic sensors that relay information to the transport bots insuring instantaneous vertical movement.

The role of the Architect thus becomes that of a programmer, biologist, chemist, and physicist. He designs the inputs for the machine and the material composition on a nano-scale, but the Arachne implements various strings of data, creating an architecture no longer predestined by the motives of hierarchical society.

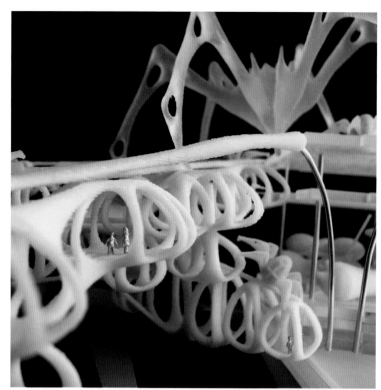

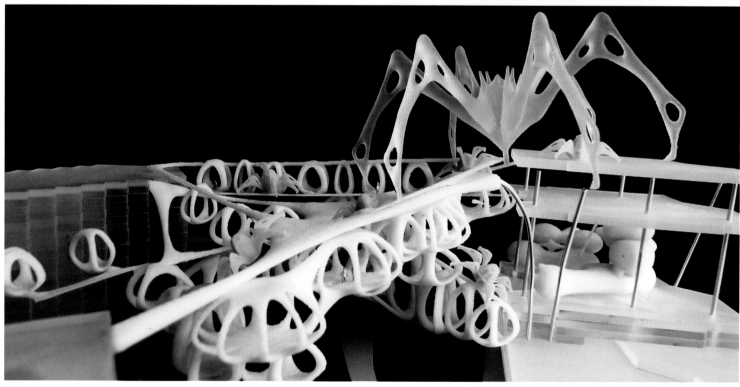

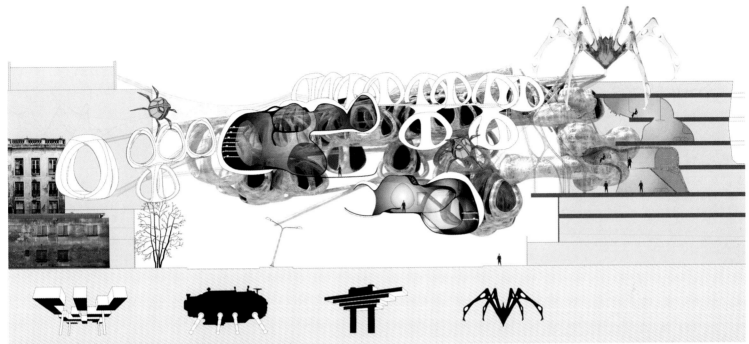

Paul Nicholls [Factory Fifteen]

Morphotic Multiplicity

Architecture is concerned with the needs of the static but has delved into concepts of multiplicity since the ornamental grandness in the baroque and rococo styles. This architecture was designed to be dynamic, to invoke movement and flow and harmony. Although the architecture itself did not move the eye would move through its undulating curves, the mind would transcend the body in the translation of form. The gold graphic of the substance in my film reflects and represents this history of ornamental multiplicity. Morphotic Multiplicity is both propositional and representational, abstract and literal. It is deliberately open-ended to give multiple directions of explorations into the uncertain, and proposes that harmony of form is achieved in the infinity of the dynamic form, or form of forms.

To see the film, please visit:

www.factoryfifteen.com/7936/151949/home/morphotic-multiplicity

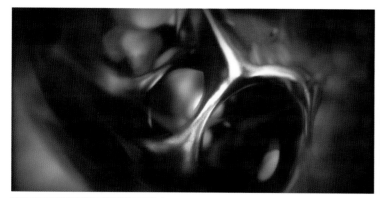

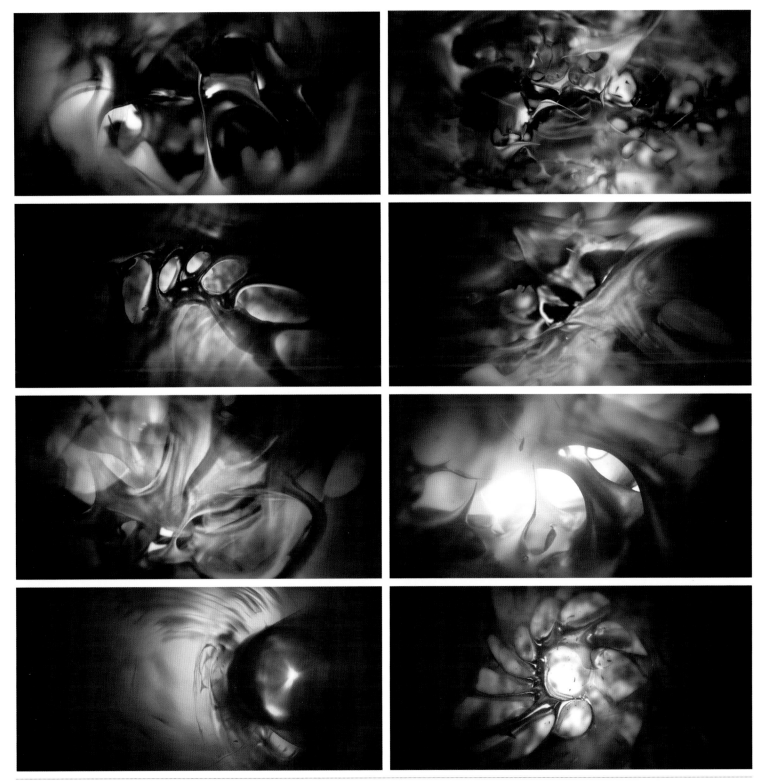

Paul Nicholls [Factory Fifteen]

Royal Re-Formation

In an age of progressively automated manufacturing and fabrication processes, the Royal Cabinets are an aggressive expression of labor. Assembled from a contractor led design approach, the Cabinets draw on highly skilled local craftsmen and artists to produce the fantastical. Staged within the proposed barren 'façadescape' of a financially fragile Canary Wharf, the Cabinets are programmatically charged with the loss of yet another great British labor force, Royal Mail.

Two ideas of labor are therefore existing in parallel. The capitalist driven one that we experience everywhere in the West, and the accomplishment of public service in a building that recounts its essence by its architecture.

The film attempts in part to graphically abstract the construction of the Royal Cabinets, in a dream-like labor of love. This abstracted reformation is a metaphor for this labor as well as representing the 'architecture of pieces' nature to the project. With the obsession for the object the film focuses on an assemblage of immense intricacy as the material slowly clusters to form the sculptural mail markets. Once formed the focus stays with the object, now in the form of the ornamentally re-branded building

parts, before the nocturnal mail markets come to life, transforming into red jewels in the urban cityscape, becoming misplaced curious objects in themselves which have a strange visual balance of fragility and aggression.

To see the film, please visit:
www.factoryfifteen.com/7936/151951/home/royal-re-formation

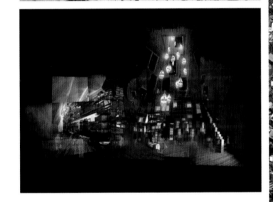

Paul Nicholls [Factory Fifteen]

Golden Age - Somewhere

Within 'Somewhere' we are transported to a time where the boundaries between what is real and what is simulated are blurred. We live online and download places to relax, parks and shopping malls. We can even interact with our friends as if they were in the same room with simulated tele-presence. Everyone is connected and immersed in nanorobotic replications of any kind of object or furnishings, downloadable on credit based systems. Distance and time become as alien as the 'offline' The local becomes the global and the global becomes the local. Consumer based capitalism has changed forever. A truly 'glocolized' world. The singularity is near. The film places us into this vision, observing an average inhabitant within the ever-changing environment of the latest SimuHouse. From a painting to a park and from a telephone call to a shopping mall. That is until there is a leak in the system and everything malfunctions. The film concludes with the house being forced to reset, giving the character and viewer a stark reminder that nothing is 'real,' not even her dog, which re-materializes in front of her.
To see the film, please visit http://vimeo.com/25678978
To visit the award winning sequel visit: http://vimeo.com/18649113

All material in Golden Age – Somewhere created and produced by Jonathan Gales, including direction, 3D/animation, post-production, audio design and soundtrack.
Client: Paul Nicholls
Animation/VFX/design: Paul Nicholls

The main creative challenge was designing the spaces. With the concept that anywhere can be anywhere, and anything can transform into anything, actually picking those places and things became very difficult. It would have been much easier if the film was site specific with traditional rules.

Technically the film posed many challenges. The transforming and particle elements required some third party plugins to achieve the desired result. The sequence where the woman materializes during an interactive skype call required filming the conversation and projection mapping the clipped sequence onto a transforming mesh in roughly the same place as the character. The compositing of graphic elements onto the 3d render and the creation of the exterior city was also quite a challenge.

To see the film, please visit:
www.vimeo.com/25678978
www.vimeo.com/18649113

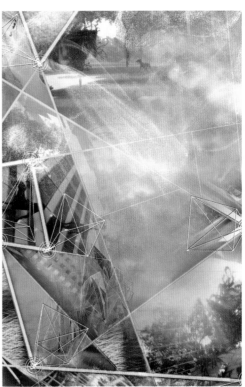

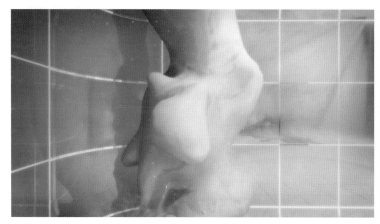

Paul Nicholls [Factory Fifteen]

Golden Age - Simulation

Memory is a fleeting thing, often constructed with fragments of objects and places in a nonsensical arrangement in the mind. Golden Age - Simulation attempts to visualize this development of memory from the very abstract to the construction of whole environments in a single strand of memory (translated as one long camera shot).

The abstract concepts explored in this short developed into a film about simulated reality, which can be seen in our project 'Golden Age - Somewhere'.

To see the film, please visit:
www.vimeo.com/18649113

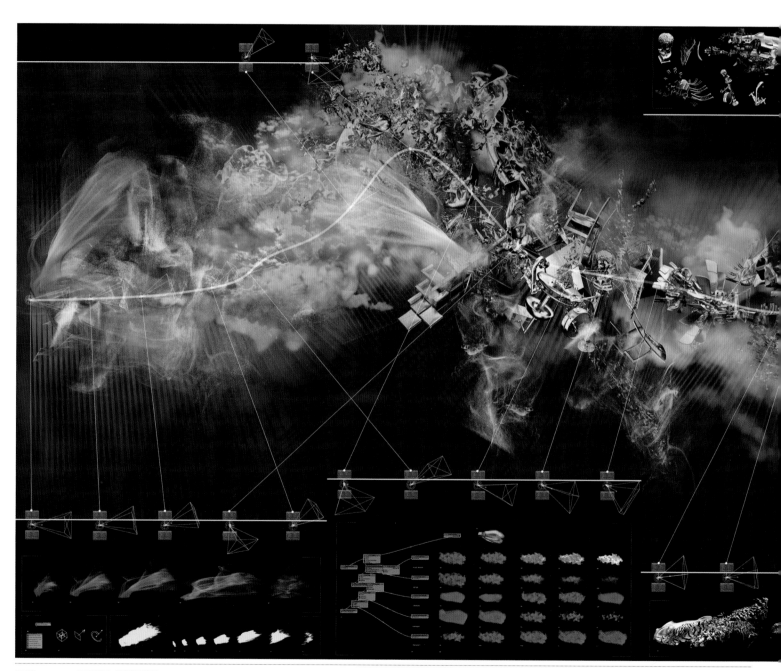

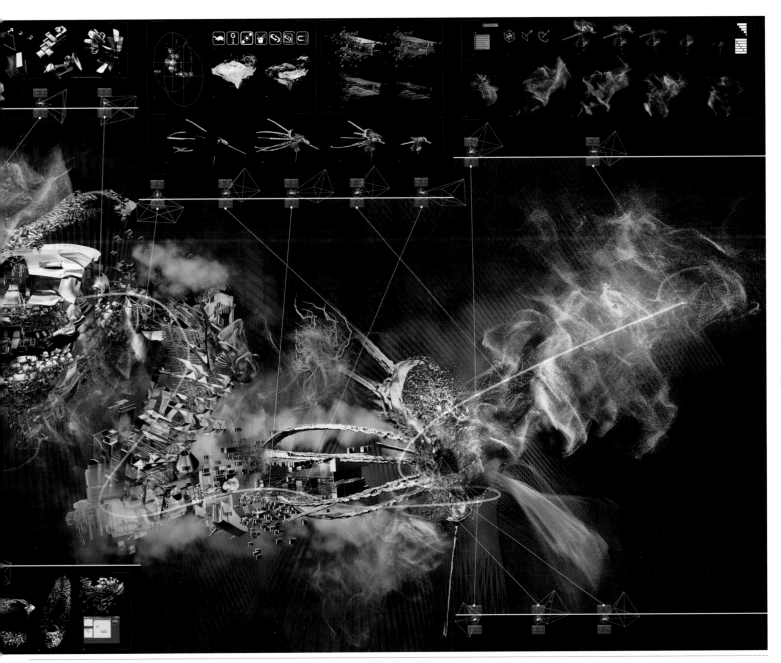

Jonathan Gales [Factory Fifteen]

Megalomania

The city is a center in terms of population and culture. It is also a concentration of built infrastructure, capital and architecture. The project focuses on the perception of the city in total construction; inspired by the incomplete state of world icons such as The Shard and Burj Khalifa. Megalomania is a short animation that explores the aesthetic of change as an ambiguous language that can be read as both growth and decay. The built environment of the city is explored as a labyrinth of architecture that is either unfinished, incomplete or broken. Megalomania is a response to the state of many developing cities, exaggerating the appearance of progress into the sublime.

The project took inspiration from Giovanni Battista Piranesi's Carceri plates, which show a fictional architecture of prison environments. The geometry that makes up the spaces within the Carceri series is ambiguous in its scale and enclosure and it could be argued that it´s impossible to build. These themes were applied to envision an exaggerated contemporary urban construction site on the scale of a city. The project began by making a series of graphics that propose new architectures in, around and stacked on top of each other. These graphics were then treated as scenes of the animation as well as becoming drawings that would stand alone.

The film contains a number of points of view and virtual camera movements, mixing between the experiential perspective of an individual alongside impossible camera positions elevated above the city. Megalomania was created predominantly using 3D CGI with some 2.5D animated sequences.

To see the film, please visit:
www.vimeo.com/25446891

1. Axonometric and elevation of 3D construction site with POV footage, generated point data and virtual camera path.

2. The construction of the city is moving at such a rapid rate that some structures are being demolished before completition to make way for large developments.

3. Sequential demolition simulation of concrete frame geometry.

4. Wireframe scene extract; demolition.

5. Cloth element. Wind simulation studies.

6. Cloth collection assigned to plane geometry to give it the physical and behavioral characteristics of cloth.

7. Wind simulated to vary in force, direction and turbulence, varying geometry movement.

8. The "Giant Wheel" elevation.

9. Wireframe scene extract; "Giant Wheel". Scene detourned from Piranesi's "Carceri" plate IX "The Giant Wheel" appropriated to the Millenium Wheel, London. The observation wheel is now a structure inhabited by parasitic architectures and ad-hoc constructions cumulatively augmenting the wheel's program.

10. First sequence to introduce the film using first person POV camera. Slowly moving along railway using organic camera movements within virtual space.

11. Train reference to "speculative landscapes"; to relate to the individual placed within a spatial environment.

12. Existing architectures to be portrayed in constant state of construction, maintainance, disrepair and demolition.

13. Second POV sequence to introduce the character to the city environment as first person explorer. Original footage choreographed, tracked, imported to virtual and developed with the *mise-en-scene* of the project.

14. Millennium Wheel detourned as Piranesi's "The Giant Wheel" in reference to the Carceri plates. The city is a vast labyrinth of construction detritus and inhabitation.

15. Speculative panopticon scene constructed from environment elements to reference "The Center of Attention" and reiterate the proposed environment as the perception of a city.

Sanne Plomp

PACC: A Space Habitat

Halfway between Mars and Jupiter lies the asteroid belt, an area with a large amount of resource-rich asteroids. This is where the project is situated. It is home to 5000 people living and working together in one space colony. This society is developed around the political philosophy of anarchism and the writings of Peter Kropotkin and Ursula K. LeGuin.

The project is an aesthetic and functional representation of the society it houses. Its societal properties, its lack of a currency, the abolition of any form of government and the absence of power concentration, together with the day-to-day activities like sleeping, working, eating and relaxing in a zero gravity environment, created the architecture.

The shape itself emerged by means of scripting, to simulate the growth of the society and its internal dynamic. Firstly the Processing scripting language was used to generate a growing pointcloud, where each point represents a type of space (varying from dormitories to industrial spaces). The growth is initiated by the population's demands for these types of spaces, basically like any SimCity type of demand model.

The spatial positioning in 3D space is based on a Diffusion Limited Aggregation system that lets spaces grow in different directions while maintaining a certain degree of clustering. Around the demand-driven DLA pointcloud an isosurface was calculated with a fixed threshold. This isosurface is the spatial representation of all the spaces combined in one structure, like skin around all our internal organs.

The DLA pointcloud did not contain any different sizes, but merely different types of points. Computational software was used to generate internal spaces inside the exterior isosurface, based on the point information. At first the raw pointcloud was remapped to better fit the society's needs. This "policy" meant for example that industrial facilities were remapped to the periphery of the structure, and that the public spaces where redistributed to the center of the building.

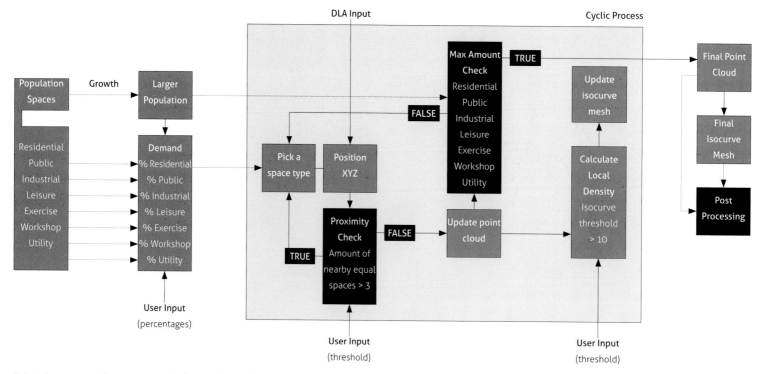

Point cloud generation process and 3D exterior mesh generation

Raw point cloud

Point cloud normalization

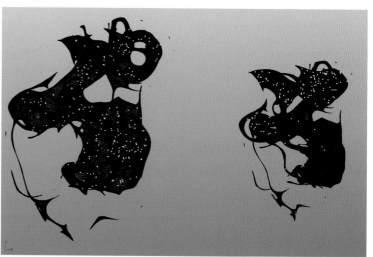

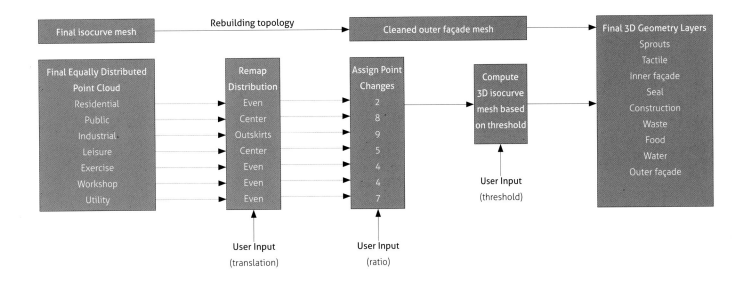

Final isocurve mesh	Rebuilding topology	Cleaned outer façade mesh	Final 3D Geometry Layers

Final Equally Distributed Point Cloud
Residential
Public
Industrial
Leisure
Exercise
Workshop
Utility

Remap Distribution
Even
Center
Outskirts
Center
Even
Even
Even

Assign Point Changes
2
8
9
5
4
4
7

Compute 3D isocurve mesh based on threshold

Final 3D Geometry Layers
Sprouts
Tactile
Inner façade
Seal
Construction
Waste
Food
Water
Outer façade

User Input
(translation)

User Input
(ratio)

User Input
(threshold)

Point cloud normalization and 3D interior mesh generation

After the remapping of the different types of points, different charges, or sizes, were assigned to the different spaces. For example, industrial facilities would be much larger than dormitories. Around this pointcloud, with a variety of charges, another isosurface was calculated, this time for the interior spaces. Between the interior and the exterior isosurface various new surfaces were generated based on different thresholds, like multiple offsets of the interior surface. This produced different layers around the interior spaces which can be used for water storage (and cosmic radiation shielding), food production, storage, building services, and infrastructure.

Processing point cloud generation script

Grasshopper interior mesh generation

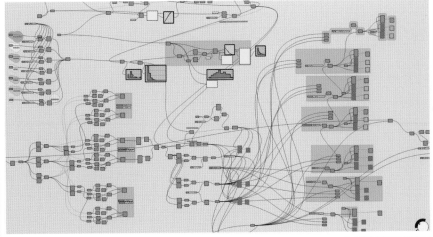

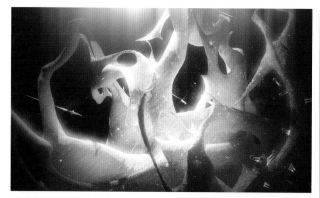

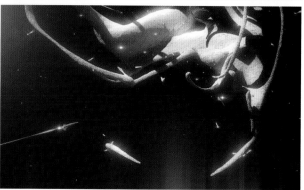

The project is an aesthetic and functional representation of the society it houses. Its societal properties, its lack of a currency, the abolition of any form of government and the absence of any form of power concentration, together with the day to day activities like sleeping, working, eating and relaxing in a zero gravity environment, created the architecture.

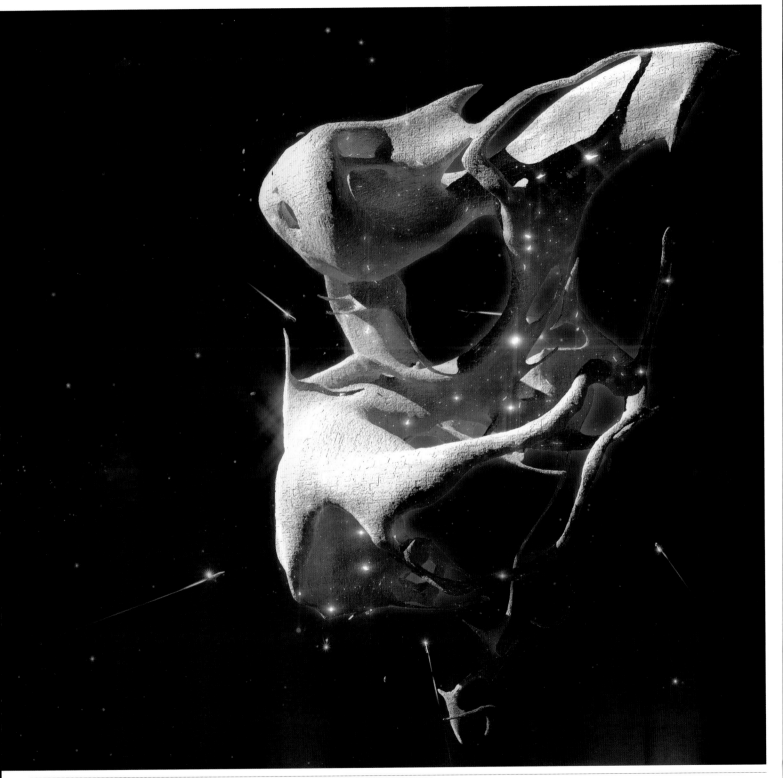

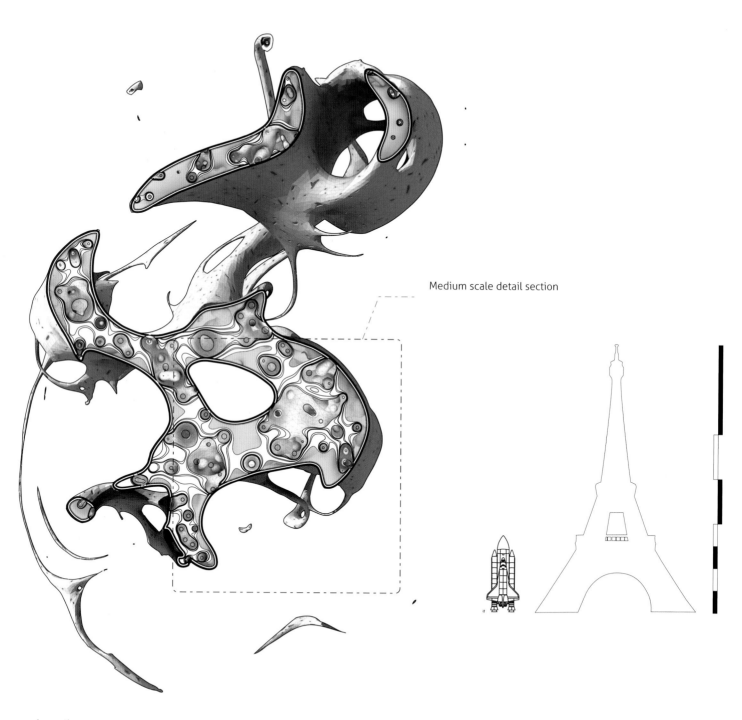

Medium scale detail section

Large scale section

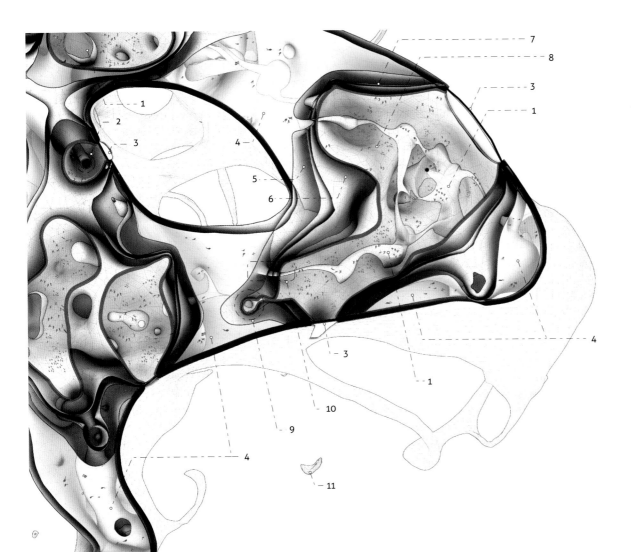

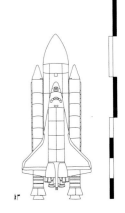

Medium scale detail section

1. **Sprout:** The sprout is a connective device that lets the user of a space connect to the shells which are wrapped around it. Depending on the use of the spaces different layers might "erupt" and become utilizable.
2. **High Speed Transportation Tube:** Some people will travel by individual thrusting, others by means of a small jetpack, and others will use the high speed trains that are available in the areas with high density.
3. **Radiation Resistive Window:** As radition is a serious problem in space, these windows will need to be protective of solar and cosmic radiation.
4. **Water Storage:** Water is the essential element for life. It is stored in large quantities as a backup in emergencies. Also the thick layers of water surrounding the spaces provide radiation protection.
5. **Food Layer:** In the food layer will contain parts for manual agriculture and for mechanized ways of growing food.
6. **Utilization Space:** The utilization spaces offer enclosed areas available for activities.
7. **Construction Layer**
8. **Large Public Space:** The large open space is a result of the high density of cell seeds, resulting in a merging of these cells. It will function as a place for public activities, gatherings but also for transport.
9. **Workshop:** Small working areas.
10. **Sprout Connection:** The connection of the sprout with its mother layer pierces through the other layers.
11. **New Settlement:** A possible attachment to the building. These small additions will gradually grow to become part of the entire structure.

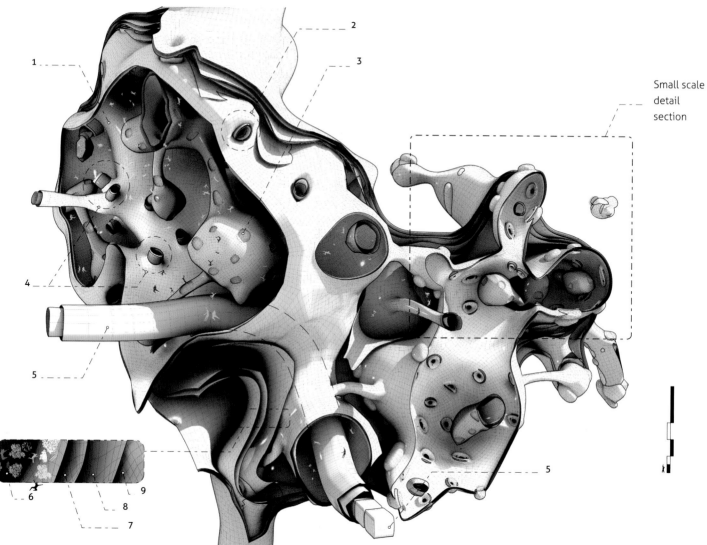

Small scale detail section

Medium scale 3D section

1. **Workshop:** These small working area's provide places for people to work.
2. **Sprout Connection:** Where the sprout connects to the layers.
3. **Sprout:** Sprout to facilitate the activities taking place in the workshop area. The layers that are needed like water and waste are usable here.
4. **Sprout Connection:** Where the layers emerge in space.
5. **High Speed Transportation:** Some people will travel by individual thrusting, other by means of a small jetpack, and others will use the high speed trains that are available in the area's with high density.
6. **Food Layer**
7. **Waste /Recycling Layer**
8. **Construction Layer**
9. **Utilization Layer**

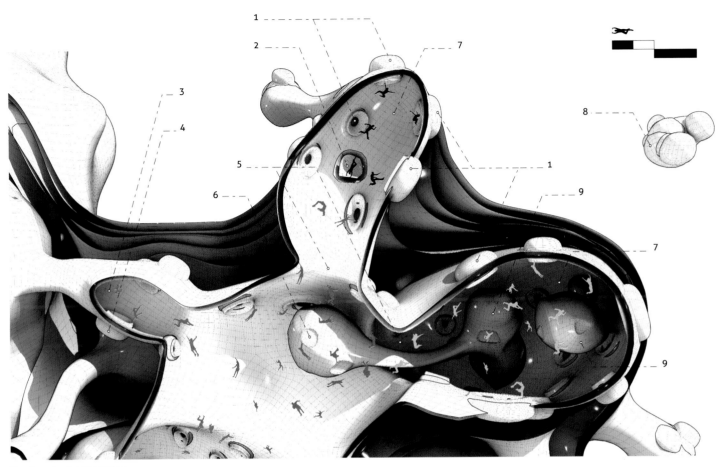

Small scale detail section

1. **Private Sleeping Pods:** These private pods can be closed off if desired. They are available in different sizes to accomodote different quantities of residents. They will contain a bed and some minor storage space.
2. **Common Sprout:** This sprout is connected to the water and waste layer to accommodate the toilets, bathrooms and kitchens.
3. **Microtube:** This connection serves for man-sized transport from one space to another.
4. **Storage Pods:** Near the microtubes are small

storage spaces for people to stow or pick up small jetpacks that help them move more quickly through the structure.

5. **Entrance To Dormitories:** The entrances to the dormitories are narrowed to illustrate the seperation of public and private space.
6. **Entrance To Sprout**
7. **Medium Sized Dormitory:** This dormitory houses around 10 people with a common sprout that contain a small kitchen, bathroom, toilet and other storage or utility spaces.

8. **Private Sleeping Pods:** This small dormitory houses 3 people and offers a large amount of privacy for those who desire it. This dormitory is connected to the larger spaces via microtubes (not visible).
9. **Sprout:** The sprouts contain small utility spaces like bathrooms, kitchens and other small storage spaces. They are are service mounts to the large layers around the spaces.

Interior and exterior mesh views

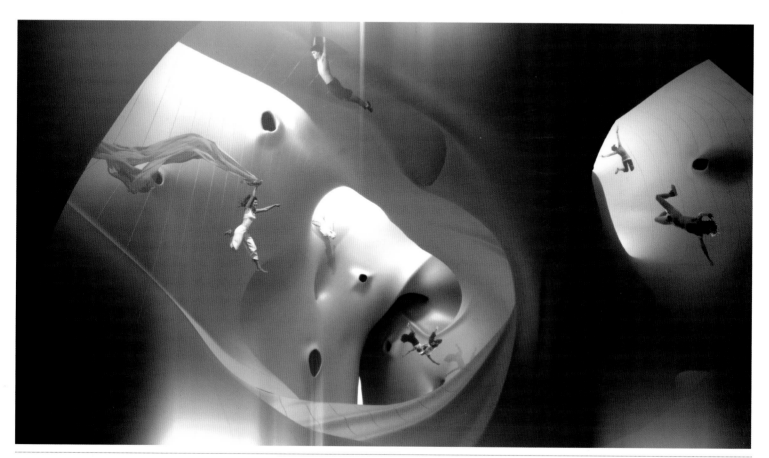

The inside of the interior spaces is not a smooth surface, but is covered with creases, folds, holds and grips for easy movement in the zero gravity environment. A colony resident moves through these spaces by thrusthing himself forward while grabbing these features on the surface. This type of self-transportation also works as a means of exercise to prevent bone and muscle deterioration common in zero gravity environments.

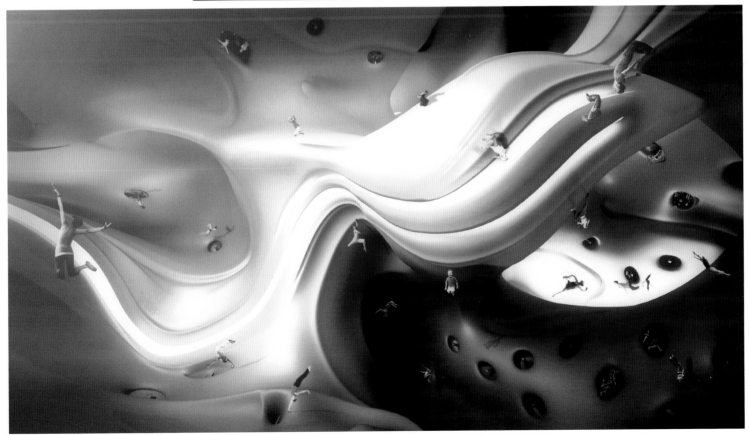